notes
to a
working
woman

OTHER BOOKS
BY LUCI SWINDOLL

I Married Adventure

I Married Adventure Journal

Celebrating Life

Alchemy of the Heart

You Bring the Confetti

Wide My World, Narrow My Bed

notes
to a
working
woman

>> FINDING BALANCE, PASSION, AND FULFILLMENT IN YOUR LIFE

Luci Swindoll

W PUBLISHING GROUP
A Division of Thomas Nelson Publishers
Since 1798
www.wpublishinggroup.com

Published by W Publishing Group, a division of Thomas Nelson, Inc., P.O. Box 141000, Nashville, Tennessee 37214.

W Publishing Group books may be purchased in bulk for educational, business, fundraising, or sales promotional use. For information, please email SpecialMarkets@ThomasNelson.com.

Unless otherwise indicated, Scripture quotations used in this book are from the New American Standard Bible (NASB), ©1960, 1977 by the Lockman Foundation.

Other Scripture references are from:

The King James Version of the Bible (KJV).

The Living Bible (TLB), copyright © 1971 by Tyndale House Publishers, Wheaton, Ill. Used by permission.

Library of Congress Cataloging-in-Publication Data

Swindoll, Luci, 1932–
    Notes to a working woman : finding balance, passion, and fulfillment in your life / Luci Swindoll.
        p. cm.
    ISBN 0-8499-4539-9
    1. Christian women—Religious life. 2. Women employees—Religious life. 3. Work—Religious aspects—Christianity. I. Title.
    BV4527.S878 2004
    248.8'43—dc22

                                                                    2004017373

Printed in the United States of America

04 05 06 07 08 PHX 9 8 7 6 5 4 3 2 1

This book is dedicated with gratitude to
six of the hardest-working women I know:

Thelma Wells,
Patsy Clairmont,
Marilyn Meberg,
Sheila Walsh,
Nicole Johnson,
and
Mary Graham.

They give me joy, hope, encouragement, laughter, and
the enormous pleasure of their company.
I love each one with all my heart.

contents

prologue

THE JOURNEY

I've been writing this book for fifty-two years. That's a long time to spend on any one project, but it's true.

From my first job at age twelve as a baby-sitter for the neighbor's children, to yesterday's speaking engagement at a Women of Faith conference, this manuscript has been forming in my head. With every day that I punched a time clock, dealt with employee problems, juggled priorities, rearranged a budget, delegated duties, arrived at work early or stayed late, socialized at a company function, flew to a meeting, or followed a career decision, I wrote another page.

I didn't know it then, but I've been quietly gathering data since I was a child. I just wish somebody had encouraged me to take notes during those early days. With a mother and grandmother who made scrapbooks and jotted comments in the margins of their Bibles so they'd know where they left off, I'm surprised they didn't insist I write things down.

Be that as it may, the minute I started thinking for myself, I did. I kept lists in little books and checked them religiously. Besides that, I'm a pack rat, so I've gathered enough information through the years to have my own database of personal scribbles with saved programs, brochures, journals, and photos. I've loved gathering information about everything, and since

I'm maddeningly detailed, I've left paper trails that have followed me around through seven decades.

Not only am I a note-taker, I'm a mapmaker. And the more detailed, the better. I find the north arrow and start in! While my parents were trying to fold a road map in the front seat, I was in the back, drawing one. I'm an information junkie. As my friends say, "Just give Luci the data, and she'll figure it out." In the fifty-odd journals I've kept through the years, I've always attached a handmade map, showing the path down which I traveled or had plans to. I like squirreling little jottings into pockets of books and clothes to get me to the right place at the right time.

The other day I was putting an old sweater into a box for Goodwill, and one of the pockets had a handmade map with this note: *Turn left on Hwy. 74 and follow that winding road. People have been known to get killed on this road so drive very carefully*—and I had put an *X* where a motorcyclist had met his Maker.

All of this information gathering suggests I've had a businesswoman's mind-set all my life. I'm glad. I love networking and brainstorming . . . being on the battlefront of business and commerce . . . taking risks and managing difficult projects . . . having an office to call my own . . . being challenged by new ideas and dreams . . . negotiating a plan to come up with the best solution . . . and being on a team. It's fun and challenging. Hard at times, of course, but I believe the benefits far outweigh the drawbacks.

If you're a woman who works, this book is for you. Or if you are just launching your career, this will help. It's possible for women to find meaning in whatever field they choose, without altering any of their standards or precepts or denying the special gift of their womanhood.

So, in the chapters that follow, I'm giving you a road map. With the turning of every page, you'll see more clearly how to get to your destination. It's out there, over the horizon, and it's your own personal niche—the work that's uniquely suited to you, whether you're a college senior anticipating a career, a mother reentering the work force, a recent graduate in an entry-level position, or a veteran who's been on the road awhile.

I frequently use the term "the Christian professional woman" or simply "the professional woman." But I'm using this term in a very defined sense. I'm not referring only to so-called professionals—doctors, lawyers, astronauts, teachers—but to the woman who sees her work as more than just a job and goes about it with a thoroughgoing professionalism.

What is crucial for true professional fulfillment is not receiving specialized training or becoming a power-driven workaholic. It's learning to think critically, evaluate wisely, and encourage the people who work for and with us without losing our sense of values. After all, there are better ways to calculate profit and loss than counting money.

I believe this concept of building both character and career has been largely neglected in the book market. And the Christian market typically has had very little to say to career women. In fact, I've noticed an interesting thing as I've researched material to bring this book to completion. Much is written for the working woman who is not a Christian: how to pull rank, how much money to shoot for, whom to hobnob with, where to go for lunch and vacation, how to beat the good-ole-boy system, and so on. We find lots of information about what the successful woman wears to work, but little is written on how to be a successful human being in that same place.

There is also a lot written for the Christian woman who is

not a wage earner: how to put the Lord first in her life and home, how to be happy if she's single, how to have a creative marriage, how to rear her children, and so on. But I haven't found much written to the Christian woman who both loves the Lord and enjoys her work.

Being a Christian woman with a career is a bit of a dichotomy to some folks; they don't quite know what to do with us. They feel the two worlds of Christianity and professionalism contradict each other where women are concerned: if you're a Christian, you should not be interested in this world's honors and rewards, and your greatest area of significance should be in your home, family, and church.

I find that viewpoint somewhat shortsighted and narrow. If you are a woman who works—a secretary, waitress, teacher, musician—a woman who rubs shoulders with others in the workaday world, you will find innumerable opportunities to utilize and convey Christian principles in that area where you spend so much time.

To go down that road is a challenge like no other. You will encounter never-ending occasions to witness, help, care, give, understand, and be involved with people who desperately need your encouragement and love. As Christian working women, our greatest calling is to love people, to line up our causes with the overall cause of Christ and allow Him to use us to effect meaningful changes in the lives of those around us. The journey to our desired destination is one of the most exciting spiritual adventures life has to offer. I know. I've been at it for more than fifty years.

So unfold your map and head out!

1 the wandering

THE AMAZING VALUE OF DEAD ENDS,
FALSE LEADS, AND ENTRY-LEVEL JOBS

The content of the job is largely irrelevant.
The point is to experience.

—Richard Bolles
The Three Boxes of Life

Gail Cox had gone for an easy one-hour hike in the woods. Dressed in a bathing suit and caftan and wearing tennis shoes, she set out on a hot Monday morning to see the wildflowers at nearby Stoddard Lake. Although the trail was rougher and more indistinct than expected, Gail was so entranced by the beauty around her—the shimmering lake, a snowcapped peak, the carpet of flowers—she stopped noticing whether or not she was on the trodden path. When she started back to her vacation cabin later that afternoon, she found herself far from the trail.

At first Gail was more annoyed than alarmed, but she became quite uneasy when her wandering continued. The terrain turned steeper and more treacherous. A sodden meadow pulled at her tennis shoes. She fell, rolled down a hill, and finally stopped herself with her walking stick.

This is ridiculous, she thought. *This is an hour's walk. What's wrong with me? Where's the trail?*

Gail was a newspaper reporter, respected by her coworkers for her common sense, remarkable memory, and quick wit. At forty, she had learned to be self-reliant, so no one had been particularly surprised when she decided to vacation alone at a retreat in California's rugged Trinity Alps. But now she herself was beginning to doubt the wisdom of the trip.

After a few hours of stumbling through the underbrush, Gail Cox had to admit, *I'm definitely lost, and I've been doing everything wrong. People who are lost panic and go in circles and die.* But Gail was determined not to die, so she slowed down and took stock of her situation.

First, Gail determined she was most in danger of heat exhaustion, dehydration, breaking an ankle, hitting her head, and having her tennis shoes fall apart. Less likely were snakes and hypothermia. And too remote to bother with were bears, starvation, maniacs, lightning, and ghosts. *Okay. I can handle this.*

It was becoming clear she'd probably have to spend the night in the woods. But at daybreak, she decided, she'd hike down to a nearby stream and wait for a rescue team—which she was sure would be dispatched when she failed to return to her cabin.

To sleep, Gail curled up on the ground and used her purse and shoes for a pillow. When she heard rustling in the bushes, she said, "Go away," in a firm voice, and the rustling stopped.

At dawn Tuesday, she found an old press release in her purse and wrote a note saying she was unhurt, "if you discount my acute embarrassment at the problem I'm causing."

There was no rescue Tuesday, although she saw a white

helicopter flying away from her over a ridge. On Wednesday morning, she decided to follow the stream, which ran down a rocky gorge filled with boulders and fallen trees. When the banks became impassable, she walked down the middle until she hit rapids or waterfalls. All along, she left little piles of stones as signs for the rescuers.

Late Wednesday afternoon, Gail came upon a small, level clearing with a pile of decaying firewood and a rusted beer can. Relieved at that sign of human life, she lay down and soon was asleep.

Thursday morning she awoke to the dying sound of a low-flying helicopter over the opposite ridge. Desperately she raced around the campsite, gathering dry pine needles to start a fire and signal rescuers. But the helicopter was gone by the time the needles finally caught.

At that point, Gail determined that helping herself was even more important than trying to notify rescuers. So she began to make some decisions. Amazingly, she found that the decision-making process itself boosted her spirits. Right or wrong, it produced the feeling of being in control.

Gail decided to spend all of Thursday at her newfound campsite recuperating—and without question, she needed the rest! By then she had a knot on her left shin, a large purple bruise on her calf, and a cut on her leg. Her lips were swollen and cracked, her big toe was scraped, and her shoulders were completely covered with insect bites. So she rested. That helped. She also discovered that if she carefully tended the fire, she could sleep an hour at a stretch all through the day and night.

Friday morning, she washed her clothes in the river, put on the wet swimsuit, and had just finished drying her caftan over the fire when a man's voice startled her: "Hello there." Turning, she saw a young man carrying a creel and fishing pole.

"I've been lost out here since Monday by myself," Gail managed to croak, "and I am very glad to see you." Her wandering was over.

Rescuers later told Gail Cox that she'd done all the right things to save herself. And she returned home more or less unscathed. But here's the most important takeaway in this story: she claims she learned lessons from her experience that she'll never forget.

For one thing, before she discards something as insignificant as a paper towel, she asks herself, "Is this something I might need?"

She also marvels at the luxuries we all take for granted, such as being able to get a drink of water without having to lie on her stomach.

And Gail is much more conscious of her own mortality. The day after her rescue, a young army reservist with survival training and experience in the mountains was reported missing in the same area where Gail had been lost. His body was found six days later at the base of a cliff.

Today Gail Cox finds herself telling people, "When you're lost in the mountains, you can either stay in one place waiting for the searchers, or you can wander around and take action to save yourself. The first way enhances your chances of being rescued. The second enhances your whole life."[1]

Nobody likes to be lost. It's a terrible, scary feeling. Being lost results in panic and fear, bewilderment and confusion, much soul-searching and wandering around to find a way out of the maze. The very definition of "lost" is thoroughly negative: "not spent profitably or usefully; wasted, attended with defeat."

Nevertheless, Gail Cox, who was lost for five days in the wilderness, reports that during that time she learned lessons about life she could not have learned otherwise—lessons that helped shape her future.

But how does her story help us?

At the very start of this book, I compared the professional journey to a road with a beginning and an end. But the truth is that we don't always get on that road right away. Many of us spend "lost" time wandering around before getting on the bus.

It's right there that we get hung up. We become discouraged because we can't seem to get off the dime. We've graduated from school, planned our future, raised our kids, so we feel we simply have to know exactly what to do. We're stymied by the attitude that if we don't charge out like a racecar in the Indy 500, leading the pack, we're failures. We visualize any wandering from the direct route to have no value.

Of course, that's not true for everyone. Some women know from their youngest years exactly what they want in terms of a working life, and with clear and singular goals in mind, they follow their dreams toward fulfillment. That happens, although I think it's rare.

Other women have a career thrust upon them by circumstances: having to be the breadwinner because of the illness, divorce, or death of a spouse; having inherited a leadership responsibility they didn't voluntarily choose; having enlisted their services in an activity that started out small and grew into a big-time operation. These people, too, may start on their path without too much wandering.

But for most of us, the career path begins down a rather circuitous route. One door opens that we find appealing, so we walk through it. Then another opens, somewhat off the beaten path, and we walk through it, too, because we feel it will add to our knowledge or advancement or both. Later, perhaps realizing that neither of these doors led to vistas that provided the satisfaction or fulfillment we were looking for, we resign those positions and try something else.

All the while, there may be a hazy goal on the horizon of our minds, but it's so far away we can't be absolutely sure it's always there or *really* what we want—it comes and goes. So we rabbit-trail, for years sometimes, in search of that ideal career or job that will provide the ultimate attainment we seek in life.

Many people call this period of time their "lost years"— the years without value or gain, the years when "I could have accomplished something but didn't." Consequently, they often view these years with regret or disappointment.

I differ. I call such a period "the wandering," and I believe it can be the most important and profitable time of anyone's life. The information gathered and the lessons learned during this interval are relevant to the rest of our careers and, more importantly, the rest of our lives.

At the most basic level, this time of dead ends, false leads, and entry-level work points us toward experience. We may not be on the career road yet, but for many of us, this is the time when we are first exposed to some of the artifacts of the working world: being on time, handling money, taking orders, relating to other people, negotiating, enduring discipline, finishing a task, and so on. Again, these are extremely basic lessons, but there's simply no way to achieve your professional goal without learning them. And they're important for living an integrated life, not just getting ahead in the working world.

The time of wandering can also teach us some important lessons about what we don't want—what's not right for us.

And these negative lessons, too, can be valuable in keeping us on the right professional road later on.

How long we wander around before getting on the path that leads to our professional niche depends on many factors. Some people settle into their workplaces and their niches very quickly; others of us wander a great deal.

It certainly took me a while to get moving in a clear direction! Just for fun, I've made a list of all the jobs I've held since I began working some fifty-two years ago, as a baby-sitter at the age of twelve. At each of these posts, I actually received payment for my duties. They are listed in the order they occurred, with a few overlaps:

> baby-sitter
> lawn maintenance helper
> door-to-door magazine salesperson
> salesperson in a variety store
> salesperson in a department store
> summer camp staff worker
> traveling vacation Bible school planner
> waitress
> swimming instructor
> teacher
> opera chorister
> soloist
> union rep for the American Guild of Musical Artists
> traveling rep for a college
> artist
> greeting card designer
> china painter
> draftsperson

> technical illustrator
> radio/TV guest
> rights of way agent
> manager of rights of way department for oil company
> editor
> speaker
> author
> vice president of public relations
> core speaker for Women of Faith

As you can see, I did quite a lot of "miscellaneous" work before developing any kind of meaningful career. During all those years, many times I felt defeated or lost. I often asked myself, *What is going to become of me? What do I really want to do with my life? How can I ever get ahead or make any money if I don't settle into something permanent?*

There were other occasions when I could feel myself on a roll. But I couldn't imagine what I was rolling toward. Little did I realize that beneath the frustrations and anxieties of my seemingly haphazard career, something was actually happening that was God-directed and important. Willy-nilly, in order or out of order, back and forth, I was learning how to cope with life's demands and deal with the issues that face each of us in our life's pursuits.

In many (I would say most) instances, I was too young to see it; therefore, the benefits from my wandering years didn't become clear to me until I was much older. That's unfortunate because each job I held taught me something about a job that was yet to come, but because of my own eagerness to move ahead or dissatisfaction with the duties at present, I couldn't perceive that the truths and lessons I was learning were going to benefit me for a lifetime of living, not just working.

Almost everything I learned in those early jobs proved of value as building blocks for later professional success. But the essentials were not clarified in my mind until some ten or fifteen years ago. Amazingly, I had written many of those lessons down in notes in my journal or little notebook each year. There it was in black and white: a lesson I learned, a trend I noticed, a change that took place. Because I had jotted a few notes, I could see what had happened even though I wasn't aware of exactly what God was doing at the time I was in it.

My own wandering occurred when I was much younger, but some women experience it later in life, particularly when they are starting out in a new career direction. Lessons learned, however, can be valuable at any age.

I used to feel that since much of what I learned about work and career resulted from wandering around without a conscious direction, it was largely unusable and unsystematizable—devoid of organizing principles. But I was wrong. I felt that much of my life had been wasted, but I was wrong.

So if you are on that same merry-go-round or live with the mind-set of defeat because you're not yet settled in the goals you hope to achieve, there's hope in these organizing principles, based on Gail Cox's experience in the mountains.

›› PRINCIPLE #1:
Don't Discard Your Scraps

Before you toss out any information or tidbits of wisdom as insignificant or useless, ask yourself, *Is this something I might need?*

I have a friend living in Seattle who is a perfect example of what I'm trying to say. A bright, charming Christian girl, she's a college graduate with a degree in communications, yet so far she has been unable to get on the right road toward her desired goal. In a letter to me she made reference to this uncertain period in her life, telling me two things in particular she's learning during her wandering years. I find this information wise for one so young.

First, get out of debt. The number one piece of advice I have for those in their wandering years is not to wander too far with only credit cards in your pocket, especially if you don't have a stable job or stable career goals.

Second, work through your personal problems. Leave that baggage behind you somewhere along the way. Then when you decide to settle down in a permanent relationship and/or career, all these unsettled issues won't come back to haunt you.

Look also at some well-known professional newspaper columnists who have admitted to "saving the scraps" of their experiences. Erma Bombeck confessed that she "had no goals whatsoever" when she began writing a column for a suburban Ohio newspaper. But her subjects—kids and carpools—wound up netting her a minimum of five hundred thousand dollars annually just because she never regarded the vignettes of her life as insignificant.

Or Ellen Goodman, a crusader for the *Boston Globe* who tracks social change and reports the process. Unlike a lot of columnists, who make use of assistants to scout ideas and clip newspapers, Ms. Goodman chooses her own subjects and does her own research. She does this because no one else knows what she's looking for. "It's mysterious," she writes. "I'm collecting string all the time." The smallest scrap of news or information might become the basis for a column.

Or there's Bea Hines, a wonderful black writer for the *Miami Herald* who says it's her "responsibility to be a watch-person for people who can't fight for themselves." Widowed in 1964 with two young sons, Hines, then a maid, answered every ad in the newspaper that said "Equal Opportunity Employer." She was finally hired at the *Herald* as a file clerk for sixty dollars a week—ten dollars more than she was making as a maid. In time, she worked up to being a staff reporter. But she acknowledges now that her experience as a maid taught her more about all kinds of people than she could ever learn as a reporter.[2] For years she's been able to use those scraps of her early experience to build a completely different kind of career. *Savvy* magazine named Bea Hines one of the top five women columnists in America.

Several years ago *Working Woman* magazine published an interesting article entitled "Designing a Corporate Image."[3] It was the story of Anne Breckenridge, who was then responsible for maintaining the interior-design image of a $7.36 billion company in Atlanta, Georgia.

The article pointed out that Ms. Breckenridge's job was the first corporate position she held after a career path that took her through more than half a dozen jobs and four states in twenty-five years. "When I started out," she acknowledged, "my basic plan was to get married, work a few years and have a baby. But then I got the biggest shock of my life—I found out that this dream doesn't happen for everybody. My husband and I divorced when our daughter was two years old."

Ms. Breckenridge told about enrolling at Berkeley's College of Environmental Design to get an MA in design—

with only a ten-year-old BA from the University of Colorado. After graduation she was hired as a junior designer at an architectural firm, only to have her experience there lead her to a better job in another state. "I've suffered several setbacks," Breckenridge said. "The job in Florida turned out to be a real dead end. Later, in a recession, I was laid off by a design firm."

But the cream of the article that surfaced above everything else was this line: "It's important to remember that rising to a great place is often—or usually—by a winding staircase."

The "winding staircase" is that unplanned path that finally leads us to the main road toward our professional niche. And the first principle of getting there is never to discard as insignificant any information along the way.

›› PRINCIPLE #2:
Don't Lose Your Wonder

The second thing Gail Cox learned from her time of wandering was to marvel at the luxuries we all take for granted. And that, too, is a good principle for uncertain times in our professional lives.

Each of us is surrounded by opportunities to become excited and involved in activities at hand. But we're waiting for the other shoe to drop. We're wanting things to get better, to lighten up, to go away. We're waiting for a ship to come in we never sent out.

During our months or years of wandering, we need to appreciate what is now. So what if we go down a false road or two along the way, or spend some time in a "dead-end job," as Anne Breckenridge called it? The sky's not going to fall—we can backtrack and go on from there. But we must never lose our sense of marvel, appreciation, and wonder. I believe this period of time gives opportunity for our hearts to expand. It's a chance to examine not only what we think about work, but how we feel about what we're doing and where we're headed.

The women who allow themselves to feel they're pursuing a wonderful career, or better stated, a career full of wonder, more often than not end up finding the niche they want, working at what they love—even when things might not seem logical or reasonable. They're the ones whose characters, not the demands of their empires, dictate their efforts. And they're the ones who find that underlying sense of purpose that's foundational to most human happiness. Wonder enlarges our vision and efforts.

This period of searching should be a time for intellectual enthusiasm, an opportunity to conduct friendly debates with those who view the world differently. Overall, it should be a time of learning to enjoy the life of the mind and the spirit, rather than having to simply tolerate what one doesn't find interesting.

>> PRINCIPLE #3:
Remember Your Own Mortality

The third principle says a period of wandering causes one to become more conscious of the impermanence of life on earth. There is something in the very act of wandering that shows us we are mortal, that nothing within us—the happiness and pain, the light and dark, the cheerfulness of childhood or the apprehension of death—settles into permanency on this earth. We're always only a moment away from the possibility of eternity itself.

Life has no guarantee that tomorrow we will still be here.

Therefore, we should say yes to the avenues that beckon us, even when we cannot clearly see where they're going. There are lessons to be learned that we can learn no other way.

A wandering period can be a very real time of prayer, trust, and faith in God—that He will provide, protect, and guide us into the exact place He wants to put us for our greatest development and outreach.

Although wandering produces uncertainty, that uncertainty can be very meaningful. Our deepest blessings can be hidden in ambivalence. Be sure of this: the wanderer is different from the person who remains at home. She tends to love more deeply and be more aware of the gift of God's provision at every turn. The wanderer is a richer person.

2 the route

IT'S ALL ABOUT BRAINS, COURAGE, HEART, AND FAITH

I am saying that both the destination and the route should be considered, and both should be interesting. We spend a great deal more time on the road than we do at the destination. Therefore, pick the best road, which isn't always the fastest. Learn how to enjoy the whole trip, the road as well as the goal.

—Fred Smith
You and Your Network

With the period of wandering behind us, and armed with the knowledge and skills learned during those years, we come to a time when our objectives must be carefully defined. In order to move forward toward our aspirations, we must ask and answer several questions of ourselves: *What is a career woman, anyway? What does she look and act like? How did she get where she is? Can I ever arrive at that destination?* We must know where we want to go and what we want to do when we get there.

Consider our target: the professional (working) Christian woman. You and I may not agree on every nitty-gritty element, but we need a broad definition toward which to aim. How about this: the professional woman is the experienced individual whose work displays exceptional quality, not only of achievement, but also of character and conduct. She is definitely not an amateur!

Added to that, this woman is one who can be counted on under virtually any conditions. She's not afraid of hard work, she treats other people the way she wants to be treated, and she works this way year in and year out. A true professional is not petty and doesn't give up easily.

I must come back to that basic thought I referred to in the prologue, because it is the key to this book: a professional woman doesn't have her sights on building an empire, but on building character.

I've observed with interest the lives of three well-known women for a number of years. Each is over fifty, and each possesses the attributes that I believe characterize a true professional. I've watched them from afar with admiration and respect and have, on occasion, sought to emulate their style and demeanor. I've read their books and gleaned much wisdom from their writings. The first woman is Beverly Sills, the opera singer turned entrepreneur; the second, a New York model named Kaylan Pickford; and the third, Sophia Loren, that stunning Italian beauty who never seems to age.

What is it these three women have that made them successful professionals and keeps them at the top of the ladder? What was the route they took that brought them to the pinnacle of achievement? What are their secrets?

I believe there are four elements vital to professional success and achievement. But before listing them, I should add that there is a distinction between success and achievement.

As Helen Hayes's mother once told her, "Achievement is

the knowledge that you have studied and worked hard and done the best that is in you. Success is being praised by others, and that's nice too, but not as important or satisfying. Always aim for achievement and forget about success." Good advice!

What are the four elements that define true professionalism? Brains, courage, heart, and faith. These elements pave the way to the building of character. They are absolutely fundamental. The longer I live and the more I'm around working people, the more I see these qualities manifesting themselves.

I've known empire builders with only brains or courage, but they don't embody enough character for me to call them professionals. They are often cold, shallow, avaricious, lonely persons whom I pity rather than admire. They may be prosperous, but to me they aren't professionals.

I've also known individuals who are all heart, with tremendous gifts of generosity, compassion, courtesy, and kindness, but who lack a willingness to change or take a risk, so they never really move on to their goals. They're too busy pleasing everyone.

Or there's the person who is locked into the idea of faith but without work—never putting the pedal to the metal. No action. No growth. No fruit.

The secret is achieving the balance of all these elements. In truly professional women, these characteristics overlap. You cannot tell where one ends and the other begins.

›› ELEMENT #1:
Brains

Take Beverly Sills. The woman has brains! I'm not saying that one must be an intellectual giant to qualify for professional status. I'm also not claiming that a college education is necessary to do well in life, although I personally feel a degree opens certain doors that cannot be opened otherwise. A liberal arts education does wonders to give us a taste of the varied world of knowledge, but it isn't mandatory for being professional. Countless women are pros who never got a college diploma; Beverly Sills is one. When I say she has brains, I mean she's an example of one who never stops learning. And she uses her head—all the time.

At three years of age, Beverly Sills was singing. By the time she was ten, she was speaking French and Italian, as well as taking piano and singing lessons. She learned classical guitar. She sang commercials and jingles, all the while avidly reading the classics and studying opera roles. By the age of twenty-three, she had learned one hundred operas. Beverly Sills had a purpose. She dreamed of being an opera star, and she used her head to pursue this dream all her life.

It's good to have dreams. Dreams are motivating. They give purpose and direction. They help us set goals, and of course goals are vital for the professional woman. But I don't list dreaming as one of the basic elements of professionalism because if we don't use our heads, our courage, our hearts, and our faith to put them into motion, that's all they are: dreams, a mental list of objectives to achieve.

Personally, I'm very goal-oriented. I operate best in a goal-oriented, structured environment because it has order and I like order. Things out of order depress me, pull my spirit down, and consequently I don't produce. Lack of order saps my energy. As my friends say, "Just give Luci data, and she'll be a happy girl. She'll get the job done!" There's a lot of truth in that. It's me.

But that may not be you, and you may still achieve professional success. I have a friend, an extremely professional high achiever, who never sets goals. She operates out of her hip pocket, and that seems to work for her. But she does have brains, and oh, how she uses them! That's why I believe that continuing to learn, using our heads, and expanding our horizons are even more important than setting goals.

Beverly Sills is the recipient of five honorary degrees. The citation for the doctorate she received from Harvard in 1974 read: "Her joyous personality, glorious voice, and deep knowledge of music and drama bring delight to her audiences and distinction to her art."[1]

What a compliment! These comments described one who has more than classroom or book knowledge—much more. They are the recognition of an individual who has applied herself to every phase of growth and learning. Her art is the radiant outpouring of her inner life and character.

Ms. Sills has never stopped growing and developing, even under the agony of family heartaches. She and her husband, Peter Greenough, have two handicapped children. Their daughter, Muffy, was diagnosed as deaf at the age of twenty-three months, and their son, Bucky, is mentally retarded. This was discovered when he was two months old.

Many women would let the anguish of even one of these heartaches wipe out all desire to go on. But not Beverly Sills. She claims she found "a kind of serenity, a new maturity" as a result of her children's problems. Her singing voice changed— became more enriched, more enriching. Her own comments convey her feelings:

> Instead of using my singing just to build a career ... I began singing for pure pleasure. I was singing not because I wanted to be Beverly Sills Superstar, but

because I needed to sing—desperately. My voice poured out more easily because I was no longer singing for anyone's approval; I was beyond caring about the public's reaction, I just wanted to enjoy myself . . . I didn't feel better or stronger than anyone else but it seemed no longer important whether everyone loved me or not—more important now was for me to love them. Feeling that way turns your whole life around: living becomes the act of giving. When I do a performance now, I still need and like the adulation of an audience, of course, but my real satisfaction comes from what I have given of myself, the joyful act of singing itself.[2]

Is that not precisely what Helen Hayes's mother told her was the distinction between success and achievement?

Beverly Sills is no longer performing on the operatic stage, but at the age of seventy-two, she came out of retirement to become chairperson of the Board of Directors for the Metropolitan Opera. After helping to revitalize the New York City Opera (the company for which she sang for decades), she began serving in 1994 as chairperson of the Lincoln Center for Performing Arts until she was called to her present position in 2002. Her interests in and love for opera never stop. And she keeps on growing even today. She comments, "I no longer have to do anything professionally or personally that I don't want to do. And as long as I am having a good time, I don't intend to stop."[3]

Don't ever stop growing! Keep using your head. Keep learning. The real obstacles to growth seem to be within ourselves. It's our responsibility to determine how we will spend our days. Will they be spent in living fully or dying slowly?

Often we find ourselves terrified at the turmoil of human life; we want to stop the world and get off. I've said before if there were just a little booth attached to the side of the world where I could go and sit and think and pray and wait until this or that problem was over, I'd be so much happier. Then, when I was better and stronger, I'd come back into real life.

But it doesn't work that way. And if it did, I'd never grow. I'd never learn. The way I learn is in the midst of turmoil, because it's not the little booth that calls out my resourceful best; it's the turmoil. Difficult times give me spiritual insight and a chance to trust God, even though that certainly may not be my choice. They pave my way toward endurance, focus, responsibility, . . . and courage.

>> ELEMENT #2:
Courage

Here's the second element that is foundational to professionalism. In late 1983 I ran across a most interesting-looking book called *Always a Woman* by Kaylan Pickford. On the front under Ms. Pickford's name were these lines:

Always . . . the greatest beauty is inner beauty . . .
Always . . . life is worth living and celebrating.

My philosophy in a nutshell—so I bought the book in a flash!

Also on the cover was a color photo of a lovely gray-haired woman with a contented, happy look on her face: Kaylan Pickford. I liked her clothes. I liked her smile, and I loved the book. I read it the day I bought it, and that night I wrote Ms.

Pickford a letter, congratulating her on her insightful writing. (This is something I often say I'm going to do but don't because of lack of time. But this time I did it, and I'm so glad.) In a couple of weeks she responded with a very kind message of encouragement and appreciation. Needless to say, I was thrilled.

Ms. Pickford is a fascinating woman. Out of intense experiences of love and tragedy and the rebuilding of a shattered life, she gives us an exciting account in her book of what can happen when a person lays her life on the line and has the courage to take risks. She tells the painful truth of how she learned to make decisions.

After ten years of marriage that produced two daughters, Ms. Pickford was divorced. Her second marriage also ended in misfortune: two weeks home from her honeymoon, and only a month following the wedding to a husband she adored, he was diagnosed with cancer. Four and a half years later, after a long and painful struggle for his life, he died on New Year's Eve 1968. Kaylan Pickford was a widow at thirty-eight.

Alone, lonely, unskilled, and grief-stricken, Kaylan had no vision, no direction, so she withdrew into herself. "In time I accepted the truth that my life would not change until I changed it. I recognized that everything I had learned and had come to understand would be meaningless if I failed to use myself. I needed to let go of inner pain, to move into life. I needed to work."[4]

Through the years, Ms. Pickford had always taken care of her personal appearance. Looking good was part of her armor to sustain a sense of well-being when times were difficult. She always wanted to maintain a vibrant physical appearance in order to project an inner strength that was reassuring to her husband and children. She claims that this not only enabled her to establish a discipline and healthy attitude when she found herself living alone after her children were grown and her husband gone; it also served as the catalyst that caused her, without references or guidance, to blindly and naively make her way into the modeling world.

She began at the age of forty-five, when everyone told her she would fail. People said an older woman would not have the vitality or the appeal of a younger woman. They were wrong. Today she is one of the nation's most photographed models. That transition began with courage.

Courage is another way of saying, "Take a risk." Believe me, it's impossible to become a working woman in today's world without risktaking. Once we determine what we hope to become, aligning our goals with our values, then we must put courage in gear to get the vehicle moving down the road.

"Experience is the child born of risk," says Ms. Pickford. "Any degree of risk has some element of the unknown, but no one courts risk without believing that there is some chance to achieve what they set out to do."[5]

Several years ago my friend Dale Hanson Bourke, syndicated columnist for Religion News Service and Universal Press Syndicate, gave me a copy of *America's New Women Entrepreneurs: Tips, Tactics and Techniques of Women Achievers in Business*. It featured comments from thirty-two women representing every business under the sun: sports, cosmetics, realty, marketing, home interiors, finance, publishing, foods, advertising, fabrics—you name it! Each gave a brief summary of how she rose to success and prosperity, overcoming odds and roadblocks, and closed her chapter with "Tips for Success." What interesting lists! I found myself making my own list of tips as I read theirs. Every woman's ideas were born out of her own circumstances in how she got ahead, and each, I'm sure, has personal value.

But here's what was so exciting to me as I read all those tips: out of the thirty-two women who expressed their ideas for achievement, nineteen spoke about the necessity of taking risks, being willing to change. Not being afraid to make mistakes, seizing opportunities. Courage.

One thing in particular Kaylan Pickford said that I found beneficial was this: "When people hear things that suggest changes in their lives, their comfort, they resist what they hear and therefore the person saying it. Only when we become committed to what we want to accomplish will change occur. We make it happen when we take responsibility for our own lives."[6]

How true, how true! But again, we must know where we're going before we can ever get on the route.

I so well remember driving to work one hot July morning in 1981, on a busy, packed Los Angeles freeway. I was praying, "Lord, I'd like to do something significant with my life. I've been with Mobil about twenty-five years, and while I'm not bored, I'd like something really exciting and challenging to fall across my horizon. Something I can do to help people. And, Lord, let me know when it happens because I don't want to miss the blessing—the fun." (Being of the conviction that often we miss the deepest joy of our prayer life because we haven't asked God to show us when we're there, I occasionally tag that last little line onto my prayers.)

That evening I was at a party at the home of my brother and his wife, Chuck and Cynthia Swindoll, who were entertaining the staff of Multnomah Press. The Multnomah people were in the Los Angeles area for the Christian Booksellers Association

Convention in Anaheim. Everyone was having a jolly old time swimming, chatting, eating, laughing—the usual fare at the Swindolls'—but as we neared the end of the party, Multnomah's publisher, John Van Diest, asked if I would stay a few minutes afterward. He wanted to talk with me about something.

When all the other guests had drifted out the door, John, Chuck, Cynthia, and I sat sipping our last cup of coffee. John said, "Luci, have you ever thought about writing a book?"

"No."

"Would you be interested in writing a book on the single life for Multnomah Press? Chuck tells me you've been single by choice all your life. Is that true?"

"Yes."

"Well, how about it? Want to write a book for us?"

I was stunned. While the idea of writing a book had, admittedly, flashed into my mind once or twice because I've always kept journals and loved writing letters, I had never seriously considered doing it. No sooner would the thought appear than I would scare it away with, *Are you nuts, Luci? What would you say in a book? Forget it.*

But do you know what happened when John presented me with that idea? It was the strangest thing. My prayer of that morning returned crystal-clear to my mind, and I kept seeing the word "significant" flash off and on in my mind's eye like a neon sign on the side of an old hotel. *Significant. Significant.*

"Naw, Lord. You can't mean *this*. I can't do this."

Then, just as clearly, the sign flashed. "Do it. This is it, Luci. You prayed about this; now *just say yes*."

So in spite of my fears, excuses, and disbelief, I heard myself saying to John, "Okay, I'll try."

Those three words changed the course of my life. I did write the book on the single life. And one after that on character, and a third one on celebration. Then a fourth on God's constancy and a fifth on adventure and a sixth . . . and on and on. And there will probably be others until God takes me home!

Since I've been writing books, *countless* doors have opened. I've had speaking engagements all over the nation, cruises, radio interviews, and television appearances. There have been hundreds of opportunities to talk with people about their careers, their lives, problems, relationships, hopes, dreams, and most importantly, the abundant way of life offered in Jesus Christ. I've made new friends and had reunions with old ones, some of whom have appeared out of the woodwork—people I thought I'd never see again and often wondered where they were. I've retired from a thirty-year career with Mobil Oil Corporation, worked for five years with my brother's international radio ministry, Insight for Living, and am now a full-time speaker with the Women of Faith core team. I've visited all seven continents and led international tours for women who want to travel. I've saved enough money for retirement, bought a home, sold it, and built a second one.

It's been wonderful! And on and on it goes, all because I took that initial risk. Because I said, "Okay, I'll try"—three little words with unbelievable dividends.

I can honestly say from experience that you have no idea what will happen when you step out in faith; when you say, "Yes, I trust You, Lord. I'm going to give this my best shot."

Of course you're scared. Of course you're quaking in your boots. Of course you're wondering about your sanity . . . but you must do it because not to do it locks you into a prison of your own making, and you unconsciously throw away the key.

With this example, look for a moment at some of the by-products of courage and how they tie in to our definition of the professional woman. Remember, Kaylan Pickford said, "Experience is the child born of risk." There's no doubt about it—I've gained a world of experience by accepting Mr. Van Diest's challenge to write a book. I like to think my writing has also improved. I'm bolder in expressing myself, not afraid to give my own opinion, which has been carved out of seventy-plus years of living.

Whenever we travel we gain experience. Remember, the person who leaves home becomes richer. We expand. We can't help ourselves. Life challenges and integrates us at the same time, giving us a broader perspective on the issues we face. We gain experience as we meet new people, increasing our horizons with new ideas, new ways of looking at situations, new focus in dealing with problems and people, new priorities in setting goals.

The actual achievement of writing that first book built my confidence too. You think I wasn't scared at times that I wouldn't finish, or that I didn't have the right stuff, or that I'd bitten off more than I could chew? Of course I was scared. Some days those feelings came in like a flood. For two cents I would have thrown in the towel—had I known where to throw it.

With writing there are so many unknowns and feelings of inadequacy. But when you're "in it" with a signed book contract, you can't just walk away or turn your back on your commitment.

Little by little, page by page, chapter by chapter, it all adds up—just as this one is doing. And one day, zap! There it is: a book. A real, bound, completed book. *My book.* That's the best part. My book. Each time I look at a book I've written, it says so much more to me than the physical object itself. It says sacrifice and work and rewrites and late nights and early mornings and love and courage and vulnerability—all those things, those qualities that make anything of value what it is.

Each time I'm invited to work on a new manuscript, I go through the same mental rigmaroles: *Well, if I did it once, why not try again? That was fun . . . well, sort of. There were tough times, but so what? There would be tough times even if I sat here doing nothing but waiting for my body to age. I'd rather be in there making a difference to somebody.*

Then I'm off again on another challenge, but stronger and more confident because I have a bit of history to back me up. That's the way it works!

The road to professionalism is not a well-marked super-highway that we traverse in the world's sleekest, hottest, latest problem-free sports car. No. This road has accidents on it and roadblocks and detours. Sometimes we're a part of those things, but we don't spend the rest of our lives there in the middle of them. We don't give up and lie down by the side of the road and say, "I'm finished, folks. Count me out. I'm not going any farther because here's a roadblock, or here's an accident." Of course not! We look for ways to circumvent situations that slow us down. We take care of the problem and move on. Perhaps we proceed a bit more cautiously at first, but don't worry—we'll soon pick up speed!

Courage enables us to live on life's exciting edge. It produces a heightened awareness and an appetite for living fully. It keeps us wondering what's going to happen next.

The peculiar thing about taking risks as opposed to not taking them is that there seems to be no middle ground. They are poles apart.

Let me explain. Most of us hate change; we fight it tooth and nail. We find every excuse in the book to avoid taking a risk because risktaking forces us out of our comfort zone. We ask a million "what if's": What if it isn't safe? What if we lose all our money? What if others aren't pleased? What if we bomb? What if we overestimate our abilities? What if "they" find out we're really faking it? (The "royal *they*," I call it, because nobody knows who "they" is, up in that mighty tower above us, and "they" are probably looking at "us," saying, "Who are they?")

So ominous is the threat of change that we submit to tedium, boredom, and apathy. Then what happens? We feel trapped. We're in a rut. Life is a grind. We hate our circumstances and ourselves . . . and often those around us. I've heard those comments over and over and over from people who want to move ahead, yet wonder why they don't. They're scared to death of risk.

Don't live your life in fear, my friend. Have courage. Believe your circumstances can change, then step out. Get at it. The philosopher Descartes wrote, "Desire awakens only to things that are thought possible." Our characters simply cannot develop until we are willing to be courageous in our circumstances. Stop holding back!

Kaylan Pickford ends her book with the line, "I risked, therefore I have." When you reach the day you no longer ignore the inner prompting, when you listen to the whisper that tells you to change, to stretch higher, to learn something new, to alter your attitude—do it. Today is that day!

›› ELEMENT #3:
Heart

When I was an executive with Mobil Oil Corporation and Insight for Living, I used what I called "the Wizard of Oz approach to management": use your brain, have the courage to take risk, but most of all, have a heart. In other words, don't be afraid to be nice.

That may sound somewhat empty at first because "Be nice" is a phrase we've all heard from childhood. Remember your mother saying, "Now when the company comes, please be nice." (At least I heard it often in my household!)

But what does "Be nice" mean? What does it mean to have a heart?

Simply put, having a heart means caring about other people. It means motivating instead of manipulating; being a nurturing facilitator instead of a hovering parent; being positive instead of negative, supportive instead of critical, enthusiastic instead of pessimistic; communicating the good news instead of calculating the bad. A professional woman with heart is a person who advocates vulnerability rather than invincibility. She's not afraid to be wrong and say so. She gives credit where it's due. She's a team player who exhibits respect and appreciation without fear of feeling diminished.

When I worked at Mobil Oil, stuck on the wall next to my desk at the office were two quotations that I had clipped from a publication called *Successful Supervisor*. It was a bulletin that floated around the building with inspirational tidbits for those who managed people. I want to pass them both on to you because they're well worth remembering and applying in our lives.

First, "Good supervision is a matter of technique, but great supervision is a matter of character. The greater your maturity and spiritual stature, the less likely you are to think of yourself, and the more likely you are to think of others, stressing the best that is in them. You get real results!"[7]

The second piece is a poem called "I Will Do More" by William Arthur Ward.

> I will do more than belong.
>> I will *participate*.
> I will do more than care.
>> I will *help*.
> I will do more than believe.
>> I will be *kind*.
> I will do more than forgive.
>> I will *forget*.
> I will do more than dream.
>> I will *work*.
> I will do more than teach.
>> I will *inspire*.
> I will do more than earn.
>> I will *enrich*.
> I will do more than give.
>> I will *serve*.
> I will do more than live.
>> I will *grow*.
> I will do more than be friendly.
>> I will be a *friend*.
> I will do more than be a citizen.
>> I will be a *patriot*.[8]

Aren't those great? Truly they are goals to aim for, and many can be reached if we simply apply our hearts to life's situations.

The concept of heart becomes especially crucial when it applies to women in management positions. I've worked for and with a number of women managers/supervisors and talked with numerous others who feel that a boss cannot be effective unless she throws her weight around, barking out orders and lording it over her subordinates. Simply because she has the power of position or title, she feels she must use it like an iron club.

But this is almost never effective in terms of getting the job done. People are rarely motivated by force. They may finish the task at hand and produce under the gun, but they'll bad-mouth the manager all the way along and find every available opportunity to undermine her efforts. The truth is, they'll hate her guts! She'll be invincible, but who cares? That kind of management says a lot more about her than it does about the people who work for her. Plus, it simply doesn't work.

I firmly believe you can convey any message gently, even if it's the worst news in the world, if you know how to say it. It's not *what* is said, but *how* it is said, that's important. Put yourself in the other person's shoes. The professional manager is a coach, a teacher, a mentor, and it would behoove many an aspiring professional woman to remember that fact, Christian or not.

If you're in a management position, are you a boss or a leader? The boss inspires fear; the leader inspires eagerness. The boss says "I"; the leader says "we." The boss sees only today; the leader also looks at tomorrow. The boss is concerned with things; the leader is concerned with people. The boss lets her employees know where she stands; the leader lets her employees know where they stand. The boss uses people; the leader develops them.

I read a bit of graffiti recently that has a lot of wisdom in it: "People willing to roll up their sleeves seldom lose their shirt." Pitch in. Help out. Do more. You'll save a lot more than your shirt!

A fellow employee told me once that I'd be a better manager if I learned to intimidate. He suggested I read the book *Winning by Intimidation* and talked to me at length about the power that intimidation would produce for me.

I never followed his advice. I didn't want power; I wanted respect. To me, intimidation creates fear and constant stress. And it most assuredly takes away a softness and kindness that I admire in a leader, be it a man or a woman, Christian or non-Christian.

Clearly, it's important that we, as female professionals, be logical (a decision-making tool that's more often than not attributed to our male counterparts). But I think it's time that we place an equal amount of emphasis on sensitivity, thoughtfulness, nurturing, and support so that the workplace is more comfortable, a place where each of us wants to spend our time and energy. And I firmly believe the result will be higher productivity!

Here are some suggestions for putting heart into your work:

> When a job is well done, give a "perk": a thank-you note (with a copy to your supervisor), flowers, lunch, a couple of hours off early, and so on.

> Maintain an open-door policy, inviting brainstorming and/or feedback on pertinent issues.
> Don't be afraid to express your feelings as well as thoughts. Encourage this openness in others.
> Learn to love and enjoy the people with whom you work. They are human beings as well as fellow employees. Inquire about their families, vacations, plans, dreams.
> Be your unique self. Don't duplicate someone else.
> Don't always act your age. Have fun on the job. Let some of the child in you show. Laugh.
> Live out your aspirations. Practice what you preach.
> Don't be hard to get along with.

This last suggestion reminds me of a comment made by Leontyne Price near the beginning of her opera career. She was featured on NBC-TV in a production of *Tosca*, and after the production was completed, she reminisced: "Well, everyone involved at NBC has become a dear friend. And one thing that was most important is that I learned professionals really don't have to be difficult to get something accomplished. You could have a very relaxed atmosphere, and *mountains* are chopped down because everybody is so pleasant."[9]

That's it: chopping down mountains together in a relaxed atmosphere. That's professionalism with heart!

One's profession is a very personal thing. It can't be inherited, nor can it be bequeathed. Only the person who puts to use her knowledge, courage, and heart with all her ability and complete dedication of purpose can truly be labeled a professional.

Notably present in a true professional are "quality of life" attributes: characteristics such as charm, tranquillity, warmth, wisdom, peace, humor, and imagination. These are the issues of the heart. They make us beautiful, although they can't be put on with a powder puff or removed with cleansing cream. The beauty of these attributes is achieved by living, loving, and learning.

One of America's most beloved actresses is Sophia Loren. Born in a ward for unwed mothers in a small town near Naples, she was raised on a shoestring and sour bread in war-torn Italy. But her ultimate professional achievements and growth seem to have been enhanced by her meager, ignoble beginnings. Craving success and love, she defied every obstacle that stood in her way, learning all the while that dedication to purpose ultimately gets you where you want to go. Through the years she has only become more beautiful.

Asked to define her biggest beauty secret, Sophia Loren replied:

It is only a "secret" because you never hear or read about it but I guarantee that it will make you more beautiful. It is a sense of inner peace . . . People have often commented on this quality that I possess, but it is only recently that I have come to appreciate what they mean. I can't take credit for it. If I do have a sense of inner peace, it comes from my history, my experiences, my mother's strength, my personal faith, my children, so many things. And any tranquility I have is fragile. There are times when I am anything but tranquil . . . Tranquility is a matter of being receptive— receptive to the small pleasures of life and to the satisfaction of goals achieved.[10]

Having a heart about our professional pursuits adds texture to our lives. It enhances relationships. It brings out the beauty of our inner souls. It sweetens our days of duties, making us more at peace and tranquil.

›› ELEMENT #4:
faith

The fourth and perhaps the most foundational ingredient that I feel is vital to becoming a Christian professional woman is faith. The Bible teaches that "faith is the substance of things hoped for, the evidence of things not seen" (Heb. 11:1 KJV).

Faith is different from courage. Courage involves stepping into the unknown with lots of questions: What's out there? Will I make it? Is it safe? Is it worth it? Do I dare? Questions about potential dangers or difficulties. It's the idea of moving forward in fear and trembling—but moving.

Faith, on the other hand, involves stepping into the unknown with no questions. It is taking God at His Word. It is trusting because He is trustworthy. It is relying on Him because we are certain He will meet all our needs. It is confidence because He doesn't disappoint. Faith is moving forward without fear and trembling because we believe God will provide.

Faith always has an object, and the object of our Christian faith is the Lord Jesus Christ, the Son of God, who goes before us in every venture. Prayer is the link between us and God. We pray through Christ to God and we believe, without question, that God hears us and sets into motion the answer to our prayers. He may say, "Yes" or "No" or "Wait." But He does hear and answer.

All this must sound terribly simplistic to the reader who doesn't embrace the same belief. And it's impossible to explain fully because it can only be perceived in a supernatural way. But it works. For Christian professional women, our faith in Jesus can clarify direction on our course; it can lift us out of defeat into victorious living; it can provide company when we are lonely; it can literally work miracles.

I say "can" because, to make it work, we must believe it will. Belief sets faith into motion. Then, when faith moves, it's amazing how our bodies will follow suit.

Beverly Sills says, "Man plans; God laughs," and there's a lot of truth to that. We can do all the planning in the world, but God knows in advance where we're headed. Why not start out by asking Him first what He has in mind? Have the faith to believe that He will direct you on the proper and best pathway toward your professional niche. That's using your head!

Kaylan Pickford refers to faith as "the child in me." She claims that because children are rich in spirit and have a natural curiosity, they have ceaseless, spontaneous ideas that keep them darting from thought to thought, like bees from flower to flower. Faith should operate like that: Always reaching out. Always trying new things. Always looking forward to what God is going to do next. Faith is activated in direct proportion to our image of God and our belief in His ability to make a difference in our lives. With faith, nothing in the imagination is beyond reach. Anything can be played out or made to happen. Have the courage to act on your imaginations.

Sophia Loren expresses it this way: "It is easy to lose touch with the spiritual side of one's nature, and this is sad because it is a great source of peace and tranquility." When faith is active, there is solace.

Whatever you do, don't allow yourself to lose contact with God. Your relationship with Him is the cornerstone to your professional achievement.

> There is ever a road that is winding
> With a signpost beckoning on;
> There is ever the glow of promise
> In the first golden rays of dawn.
>
> There is ever a friend that is waiting
> To guide and encourage with love.
> With cheer like the sunlight streaming
> Through our darkest sky above.
>
> There is ever a hope that is glowing
> And inspiring our efforts anew;
> Ever the goal that we cherish
> That gleams in the faraway blue.
>
> There is ever the prayer that is whispered
> For the joy tomorrow may bring;
> There is ever the faith to sustain us
> Till we find our beautiful dream.[11]

3 the signposts

YOU'RE GETTING SMARTER ALL THE
TIME—GUARANTEED

*Thus in the beginning the world was so made
that certain signs come before certain events.*
—Cicero
De Divinatione

One of the joys of growing older is that life validates what we already know but have been unable to define. As frequently as we may have backtracked to find our way and felt we were starting over in the same old place, we were, in truth, not in the same place at all. At each juncture of "beginning again," we are a little wiser than before, and that modicum of wisdom, learned from experience, makes all the difference. With each step we grow.

Growth doesn't come easily. There are peaks and valleys, good and bad days. But all the while we're slowly moving ahead, changing for the better. That's what's important. As my brother Chuck says: "Growing and learning are healthy, normal experiences. Both have to do with a process . . . and that process is sometimes painful, often slow, and occasionally downright awful! It's like taking three steps forward and two steps back."[1]

That third unrepeated step is the one of victory that emerges out of the tough, incessant, daily struggle of trying to keep one hop ahead of the hounds.

Rarely do we know with pristine clarity what we want to do with our lives at every given moment, because of the variables. And almost as rarely are we able to take stock of our progress, because we don't know where we are in the overall scheme of things. Are we in the middle of the journey, near the end, or still dillydallying somewhere around the starting gate? It's difficult to calculate progress without signposts. Therefore, I suggest we establish signposts on our professional journey that will both mark our way and advise us what to do next.

›› SIGNPOST #1:
Anticipate

As we discussed in chapter 2, true professionalism requires courage. A working woman must have the conviction that her life is going in a particular direction toward a desired destination. To arrive there she needs to use her head *and* her heart, weaving a delicate web of work, caring, learning, risk, and faith in order to give her stability and purpose in the midst of this pursuit.

I'll go a step further. The professional woman must learn to anticipate her future—when to defer rewards, when to expect rewards, when to back off, when to move ahead, when to wait. She needs to develop a sense of timing.

If only there were flashing neon lights on our professional road warning us not to take the alternate route or warning that there is trouble ahead. But we don't have that visual advantage. Therefore, to the degree that we're able, we must train our powers to anticipate what lies ahead so that we'll know when to shift gears in advance.

What does the future mean to you? For many of us it means a time of reward. We work hard, make plans, and put off immediate gratification in order to have something of value later on. To achieve future rewards, it's important to learn that everything cannot be had now. The richest life has a lot of waiting in it. And I don't mean "sit, soak, and sour" waiting. I mean present investment for future fulfillment. Working hard now to earn credentials later. Turning our dreams into reality by making use of present possibilities.

This is one reason I value higher education. Time spent in study and preparation trains us for secondary reactions, not just immediate actions. By the simple discipline schooling requires, we learn to extend response time and delay gratification. Our diploma doesn't come at the end of today's work or tomorrow's tests, or even after the investment of one year. It's the outcome of years of endeavor. The educated individual is usually willing to postpone gratification in anticipation of a better reward down the line. This is very important, because the rewards that come over time are generally more bountiful than those received at the end of this hour or this week or this month.

Learning to anticipate also teaches us something a bit subtler. The best choice won't always feel like the right choice, but by anticipating blessing in that decision, we develop the strength to accept where we are, live through it, and go on. Three steps forward, two steps back.

A few years ago I took a "lifeline" test printed in *The Executive Female* magazine. It was a graph on which the participant was to draw a mean line representing her life from birth to her present age. Above or below that line she drew another line showing major turning points in her life: jobs, marriage, divorce, schooling, successes, failures, and so on. The line moved up and down as it ran from left to right, according to how well things went at a given time. If the years or experiences weren't very good, the line sloped downward, below the mean line. If they were really bad—the pits—the line dipped very, very low. And the reverse was true for the good and very good years.

Interestingly, when I finished drawing the graph, I noticed a revealing truth about my life. First of all, very little was near the mean (or average) line. Most of it was above or far above. But there were two occasions, one in my early twenties and one in my early forties, where the line dipped very low.

The two lowest points in my life I remember well. The one in my twenties had to do with the pains of individuating, becoming my own person, and discovering my own identity. The one in my forties was related to the difficulties pertaining to moving into a new job and new surroundings where there was no turning back.

In both cases I felt trapped, unable to get out from under the psychological load that had landed me in both places. I experienced a loss of personal control and a gnawing torment in my spirit. I felt terrible all the time and constantly agonized until my circumstances changed.

In looking back now, however, I see the irony: the most profound lessons I've learned about life were the by-products of those two very low times. The circumstances didn't change until I got sick and tired of fighting myself, my ego, my dilemma, and God. One day I simply said to Him, "Okay, I'm fed up. Do what You want to." Then He did. Almost immediately things got better. *Finally* He had gotten my attention, and I shut up.

Those occasions taught me that while life is capricious and unpredictable, often not what I want it to be, it is always within the scope of God's plan and purpose. What I thought was an absolute dead end was actually God's fertile proving ground. I hated it. But the principles learned then are the ones I use every day in dealing with both myself and other people. Those experiences demonstrated that no predicament is beyond God's light. My darkness is His opportunity to shine.

Notwithstanding these facts, not every reward need be deferred. Some of the sweetest rewards are for now, and we should anticipate them daily.

Although I knew the truth of Scripture and had experienced the presence of the Lord countless times prior to reading my lifeline, when I saw the benefits in my human impasse, the realization of His unending provisions seemed to have renewed redemptive value. I felt one with Him. I was reminded of the loving nature of God—that He cannot make a mistake with my life. He promises me success, prosperity, courage, and strength as long as I obey His Word. He commands me to tell other people these truths. When I do this, I can anticipate His presence on a moment-by-moment basis every day.

God speaks to us as He spoke to Joshua:

> Only be strong and very courageous; be careful to do according to all the law which Moses My servant commanded you; do not turn from it to the right or to the left, so that you may have success wherever you go. This book of the law shall not depart from your mouth, but you shall meditate on it day and night, so

that you may be careful to do according to all that is written in it; for then you will make your way prosperous, and then you will have success. Have I not commanded you? Be strong and courageous! Do not tremble or be dismayed, for the LORD your God is with you wherever you go. (Joshua 1:7–9)

The promises of God and the power of His Spirit are mine to rely upon without ever waiting. No deferment. No postponement. They are a breath away, and for the problems that face women in the workplace, that's great news. As one woman has said, "Don't be afraid of tomorrow; God is already there."[2]

›› SIGNPOST #2:
Yield

We've all read Murphy's Laws, and no doubt, we've seen many of them in action. There seems to be one to cover every conceivable situation. They're funny because they're so true.

For example, "If there are two events of importance, they will always conflict." Haven't you thought that on the night two of your favorite movies were being aired on television at the same time on different channels? There are other old laws to live by that bear repeating:

Blake's Law:	The longer you save something for future possible use, the sooner you need it after it's destroyed.
Roe's Law:	No matter what happens, somebody knew it would.

| Childer's Law: | When everything is perfectly clear to everyone, somebody didn't get the message. |
| Donsen's Law: | The specialist learns more and more about less and less until he knows everything about nothing. |

Which brings me to my own law:

| Swindoll's Law: | Leaders who always have to do the job themselves often do a job on themselves. |

Show me the leader who has never learned to delegate, and I'll show you the leader headed for burnout or an early grave. The fine art of delegation is one of the major keys to professional success, but many people would rather drown in a sea of paperwork, simply because they fear disaster: "If I don't do this myself, it won't be done right." And they wonder why their staff looks bored to death.

Delegation implies mutual commitment. Delegating responsibility says, "I trust you. You are an integral part of this organization. Your success is our success." Even though all textbooks preach the virtues of delegation, rare is the manager or supervisor who delegates as a routine way of life. There are many reasons for this:

> It will take longer to teach someone else to do it than to do it myself.
> This is so important that it requires my personal attention.

> If I do it myself, I minimize risk.
> What if I lose control of the job?
> What if she does a better job than I would do?
> What if there are errors?
> I might appear lazy if I give this to another person.
> Others will think I'm too close to my staff.

Sound familiar? Of course. Not only have we heard these reasons; if we've been in any kind of management position, we've said them ourselves.

But do you know from what source those words spring? From the empire builder. The empire builder always fears looking bad, losing control, risking repercussions. The woman who isn't interested in an empire, on the other hand, views delegation as an opportunity to teach and mentor as well as a practical measure to free her time for other areas needing attention. The paradox of delegation is that "the more often you delegate, the more committed you are to working with people. The more you give away, the more you take hold of your operation."[3]

One of the greatest gifts you, as a manager, can give those you manage is to teach them to become autonomous. Autonomous individuals function on their own motivation, not yours. They don't feel manipulated. They are not peripheral, but integral in the network. Their feedback and brainstorming become unique and creative.

And mark my words: not one person above you will think you're lazy. On the contrary, your supervisors will be amazed at the team spirit, the high morale, and the enjoyable atmosphere that emanate from your department. You'll see a level of production that you'd never know otherwise, because everybody will be working where the action is, as team players toward joint goals. It will be motivating. It will be contagious. And best of all, it'll be fun. It all starts with yielding some of your control.

I know that you can't delegate everything in the scope of your responsibilities. Some things only you can do because they have to do with your particular gifts, talents, training, or expertise.

When I'm invited to speak, for example, I can't send a substitute. I'm me, and I have to represent myself. Similarly, when a professional lawyer or doctor or performer is hired to do a particular task, there can be no delegation.

But in cases like that, that's another kind of yielding. When I accepted the challenge to write this book, there was no way for me to delegate that responsibility. The task was mine. This book had to be composed of my thoughts and philosophy about professional women, gleaned from my own life and experiences. Being accountable to my publisher for that commitment, and being unable to delegate any of the work, I then had to go to step two of yielding. I had to relegate the activities related to writing a manuscript to a certain order of action and accomplishment.

This book has been a long time in the making. I've done research, studies, interviews, questionnaires. I've written at times when I'd rather have been playing. I've said no when I wanted to say yes. I've put various other involvements on hold. I've set scores of "mini" deadlines to check my progress.

So my motto is, *When you can't delegate, relegate!* That's the only way in the world the busy person accomplishes anything. Even then, flexibility is the name of the game. We must be willing to yield in order to avoid collisions ahead.

>> SIGNPOST #3:
Caution

Lily Tomlin said, "For fast-acting relief, try slowing down." No doubt, the most difficult question for the working woman to answer is this: When is enough, enough? It's the haunting refrain that plays in our heads when we're not through with a project but we're dead tired; when we've been offered a better job with a bigger title and more money but the present position has nearly killed us; when one more sale, one more late night of work, one more trip out of town away from our family and friends will surely put us over the top. When is enough, enough?

It seems to be characteristic of high achievers to choose what is good for advancement but impoverishing for the spirit. We may be well rewarded and surrounded by possessions of quality but find ourselves in a spiritual vacuum, with inner feelings of emptiness. We have paid for our acquisitions with the loss of emotional and spiritual equilibrium. We simply want too much at the expense of our sanity.

In his fine book, *Modern Madness: The Emotional Fallout of Success*, Dr. Douglas LaBier writes, "Passions for fame, power, and money, when they come to take over the person's reason for being and become ends in themselves, constitute forms of insanity."[4]

He points out that the most common consequence of this conflict of values is a feeling of self-betrayal. By embracing "careerism" with its perks and payoffs as a way of life, these "self-betrayers" have forfeited a life of meaning and integrity. They've given up something of themselves and now live with festering questions and self-criticism. He goes on:

The new-breed careerist suffers emotionally when he or she makes decisions and choices which are bad, in the sense of limiting or distorting personal development and inner sense of meaning, although they seem attractive at the time because they are good for the career. Some poisons can taste good, but will still make you sick or kill you.[5]

What we're talking about here is balance, that wonderful stability we admire in others yet find so hard to achieve in ourselves.

The worrisome and somewhat surprising fact is that statistics show men are less likely than women to be married to their careers.[6] Somehow, we women see ourselves as forerunners to a new wave of opportunities. We have to keep forging ahead to blaze the trail for the next generation of women. We're the pathfinders, the pioneers. So without conscious realization, we seek to outdistance each other, damaging ourselves in the process.

It's all too easy to lose perspective. Therein lies a sinister, blinking danger signal. Typically what happens is that the emphasis on competition produces such a strong desire to succeed that we sacrifice our sense of well-being for it. We work hard because we must, without time for other interests. Then later, when perhaps there is time to develop the balance, we find our careers are more rewarding than any other aspect of life, so we continue to lose ourselves in them. We never develop another life, nor do we stop long enough to tell ourselves, *This is enough!* And corporate structures are typically designed with policies that encourage such a loss of personhood for the benefit of achieving.

I worked with a woman like this once. Eager to prove herself worthy and ambitious to move ahead, she demonstrated a workaholism that surpassed any I've ever witnessed. She came early, stayed late, and on occasion even spent the night on a small sofa in the ladies' room so she could work as many hours as possible. She had no life apart from the office. The pity was that the more she worked, the less she seemed to catch up, much less get ahead. She became a frazzled, sleepless victim of a "modern madness" to achieve success. She betrayed herself and everything she wanted. Ultimately, because her work reflected more chaos and confusion than caring and control, she was fired—an embittered, tired, resentful woman.

This is an extreme case, I know. But wherever you are, if your whole life is work, you are walking into the same insidious psychological trap. It's so easy to get caught. Read the signposts along your professional road, and take heed. Remember, one's obsession with work doesn't come from the organization; it comes from oneself.

One of the sad, deceptive results of this type of ladder climbing is that when we're in a management position, we begin demanding the same commitment from our employees. Because we made it to the top by working around the clock, we think others should do the same. Generally, workaholics make rotten managers!

Well then, where does the balance lie? How can I create private time for myself with such an impossible schedule? How can I replenish my spirit? How can I know when enough is enough?

Gail Sheehy, the author of *Passages* and *Pathfinders*, tells us: "Would that there were an award for people who come to understand the concept of enough. Good enough. Successful enough. Thin enough. Rich enough . . . When you have self-respect, you have enough, and when you have enough, you have self-respect."[7]

Excellent—and oh, how true! Self-respect is the key to knowing when you have enough. It opens the door to personal satisfaction and a sense of fulfillment. When you love yourself and accept yourself for who you are, you have nothing left to prove.

With a little work, a little practice, and a lot of determination, you can develop the self-respect needed to pursue excellence. There's only one prerequisite, and it's a major: *You must want it!*

Keep in mind that no one else can give you balance and self-respect. They are already inside you, waiting to be discovered and developed.

Look at it this way: Everyone is born with muscles, and everyone uses them. However, some people use them more than others. If you're willing to use your muscles—to exercise them with regularity and follow a sensible, ongoing program for muscle development—you will become a healthier person, more in tune with your body. The same is true for the development of self-respect. Your willingness to commit yourself to shedding self-doubt in an ongoing program of development will make you a more assured, confident woman.

To reach this state of self-respect, try these ideas on a consistent basis:

1. *Develop your own style* . . . in your grooming, tastes, furnishings, stationery, business cards, ideas. Become your own person, an original, not a copy of someone else. Be creative.

2. *Work on your weakness.* When you spot short-comings in yourself, don't be afraid to admit them. Apply elbow grease to bring about change.

3. *Never give up.* What stands between mediocrity and excellence, between failure and success, are four words that lie within you: "I can do it!" Set your sights on goals for self-improvement and keep working toward them. Do things. Be decisive.

4. *Don't be afraid to ask questions.* We get where we're headed by inquiring about things we don't know. Find answers. Make mental notes. Don't let not knowing intimidate you.

5. *Admit when you're wrong.* Nobody's perfect, and nobody wants to be around someone who thinks he or she is. Ms. Perfect is a pain in the neck, so be vulnerable.

6. *Develop hobbies and be actively involved in them:* reading, gardening, music, skiing, painting. Thousands of enjoyable projects outside work are waiting for you to bring them to life. Never lose your sense of wonder; let life be wonderful.

7. *Trust the gifts God has given you.* Each person is made uniquely. Use your talents without holding back, and bring them to bear on all your experiences and decisions. You may discover gifts you never thought you had.

8. *Be compassionate.* Thank other people for who they are and what they do. Show mercy and tolerance. Don't be afraid to give your money for a worthy cause. Be generous in spirit and pocketbook.

9. *Laugh a lot.* Don't take life and your situation too seriously or literally. Recognize that tomorrow's another day—bad things don't last forever.

10. *Daily commit your energies to the cause of Christ.* Say yes to the doors He opens. Spend time talking to Him, praising Him, thanking Him, and learning about Him. Walk by faith, believing He can and will bring you to maturity.

>> SIGNPOST #4:
Slow

The time comes in every professional journey when retirement has more appeal than the racetrack. Eventually it's time to slow down. For some of us that time is far in the future, for others just around the bend, but we would all do well to keep it in mind. As we negotiate this last leg of the road, there's no need to stop as long as our health remains, but there are reasons to rest more often, reflect on where we've come from, and teach others about what to expect.

No matter where you are on the professional road, it's a good idea to get in touch with who you are now so that during your quieter years you can enjoy the companionship of yourself. At the same time, keep making new friends and enjoying new beginnings. Stop regretting endings. Life is full of change, crises, faded dreams—we know that by now. But those of us whose "life is hid with Christ in God" (Col. 3:3 KJV) will never run out of hope or the deepest kind of peace. Don't be afraid to sacrifice, remembering you can keep only what you give away.

Forgive yourself for the errors of the past, and put them to rest once and for all. We've all made them. So what? Don't carry the weight of that guilt one more day. Dump it, and leave it behind you. Leave that baggage on the road somewhere. Life is the process of discovering who we are and what we can accomplish. As we read the signposts and interpret them for ourselves, we understand where we're going. We learn what is possible and what is not.

Eugenia Zukerman, the professional flutist, gave us this thought: "Learning is a procedure which evolves. If someone could give you that magic formula which would make you instantly a fine artist, you would be bored. Discovery is so important in your work, in relationships. In everything you do. It's the process that's important."[8]

And the process of discovery will continue to lead us from signpost to signpost on the road to our professional niche.

4 the roadblocks

*By now it should be clear that pathfinders
are not magically shielded from surprise
bumps in the road.*

—Gail Sheehy
Pathfinders

Sometimes I'm dumber than I look. The truth of that con-
fession was brought home to me one day on my way to work.

Twenty-six miles of roadway lay between my home and
office. I drove that stretch daily, so I knew it like the back of my
hand. Most of it was freeway, but for the last four to six miles
I had to thread my way through surface streets. For a period of
five months or so, those surface streets were in chaos. The
cities through which they passed were in the process of
installing a massive underground sewer pipeline from point A
to point B, and it seemed to me point A was just about where
I left the freeway and point B, somewhere beyond my office.

Everything was torn up. There were trenches, metal plat-
ing, bumps, potholes, blinking warning signs, and traffic jams
you wouldn't believe. All this confusion was intensified by

gigantic pieces of equipment with enormous tires and cranes and scoops and buckets, which came along to open the earth, fill it again with the pipeline, compact it, then apply asphalt . . . while I waited.

Needless to say, tempers flared. Horns honked. Rude gestures flashed back and forth. One day the people in the car behind me became so mad at the signalman who was showing favoritism to a car full of guys he apparently knew, they cursed at him and got out of the car, grabbing handfuls of rocks to pelt him with when they got within throwing range. I was mesmerized by the scene, but unfortunately the light changed and I had to scramble ahead, leaving an impending murder.

Like everyone else, I was sick of the whole thing: roadblocks, complications, the delay in getting to work. Every day, just to hear my head rattle, I asked nobody, *Is this ever going to end?* My rattling head answered back, *Of course not, you fool. If it ever does, you'll be too old to drive.*

That became my daily diatribe: *Is this ever going to end?* Those six words ruled my morning from point A to B. I dreaded going to work because I hated those final few miles.

One day I arrived at work out of sorts and mad at the world. I walked in—late, of course—and was mouthing my disgust with my unwelcome plight when one of the fellows I was dumping on said, "Why don't you come to work a different way?"

"What do you mean? There's only one way, and it's through that mess."

"No, Luci," he said. "Don't turn off 91 onto the surface street. Keep going until you meet up with the Harbor Freeway where 91 ends. There's a huge intersection there, and it's much less congested. I come that way every day."

"Hold it. You're telling me there's no bottleneck at 91 and Harbor? You're crazy. I used to go that way, and it was such a tangle I switched over to surface streets."

"Well, that hasn't been the case in four or five months," my friend said. "Everybody must be going the way you are. Tomorrow, come to work my way, and check it out. Even if it's congested, it surely doesn't have all the congestion you're usually caught in."

Where had he been all my life? Duh! The next day I switched routes, and the words *Is this ever going to end?* were replaced with *Why, this is the smartest thing I ever did.*

Somehow, unwittingly, I had gotten in a rut, feeling there was no way around it, hating it, griping about it, getting out of sorts over it, when finally someone called my attention to the fact that it didn't *have* to continue.

There was a way around those roadblocks. I just hadn't thought of it, as dumb as that may sound.

It's not always easy to be smart, think smart, act smart. We get in ruts—bogged down, blocked. And we stay there because we can't figure out how to get around whatever is keeping us from progressing.

The truth is, there are ways to maneuver around almost every roadblock in life, even if this means nothing more than changing our attitude so the roadblock is easier to cope with.

Besides, roadblocks are wonderful character builders. They help us grow up because they make us mad, and when we get mad enough, we generally set about to change the situation.

My mother used to say, "Nothing changes until we get sick of ourselves." Development and growth often spring from those things in our lives or circumstances that we can no longer tolerate. Being blocked makes us take action. We search

for a way around or out of our unwelcome plight. And sometimes we simply need a friend to suggest an alternate route.

For the woman who holds in her heart the dream of being
a pro at what she does, it is impossible not to face roadblocks.
We need to know this at the outset. At times roadblocks seem
to appear out of nowhere. They're constructed by other people
or society or tradition, history, the norm. Even stress. Often,
we build them ourselves!

The longer we ignore or accommodate roadblocks, the
greater a problem they become. But we don't have to let this
happen. Roadblocks are like bad habits that, when recognized
and called by name, can be changed with the help of God and
determination. Just keep in mind when you come up against an
irksome barrier that it is designed to build character, not
destroy it.

The problem is, we tend to want these situations changed
now. We're sick of the obstacles, and we want them out of the
way immediately. But that's just not the way most problems are
solved. More often, change comes by facing one day at a time.

Let's make that into a six-word slogan: *Face one day at a
time.* That's how anything is accomplished. There are no
overnight cures. Before we can reach the goal we hope to
attain, we must go down the road from point A to point B, even
if it takes a bit of supernatural strategy getting around the
roadblocks.

In the musical *The Wiz*—a saucy, jumping takeoff of that
immortal fantasy *The Wizard of Oz*—there's a song sung by
Evillene (the Wicked Witch of the West) called "Don't Nobody
Bring Me No Bad News." It's terrific, and if you could plug
earphones into this book and I could sing it to you now, I
would, because it fits so well with what I'm saying. It's what I

often heard in my head when I fought that daily battle on the way to work. *More bad news!*

Sometimes we get the blues over roadblocks—and not only the blues, but downright discouragement. We want to look at the world and say, "Don't bring me that news, baby. It's baaaad . . . and I can't take it. I'm sick of it. One more piece of it, and I'll be done in!"

But there are ways around it; there *is* strength to go through bad news. And one way is to do things minute by minute, one day at a time, not biting off more than we can chew.

In my years of working in the corporate world, I met and got to know executives and managers of all types, and in my fifteen years of professional singing with the Dallas Opera, where numerous stars and superstars crossed my path, I had opportunity to observe a great many individuals. I've seen the ways in which a wide variety of professionals dealt with obstacles. I've also had my own personal experience with roadblocks.

The interesting insight I've learned from all this is that most roadblocks in my career are the same ones faced by people of much greater influence and stature than me. Almost everybody comes up against these common barriers at some point or another. So out of the seedbed of my observation and experience, I'm here to tell you that roadblocks *can* be overcome. I want to suggest a few ideas for getting around those that we most frequently encounter.

›› ROADBLOCK #1:
fear of failure

The greatest roadblock of all in the life of almost every person I know is *fear of failure*. This is a dogmatic statement, but I believe it's true. This fear may take different forms, so it is sometimes difficult to recognize. But even the greatest men and women of history have had to struggle with feeling helpless and afraid, confused or infantile—or so historians later recorded. Rare is the leader who does not at some point become convinced that he or she has failed.

Most people like to excel, not just please, but do the very best they can. As my brother says, we want to live above the level of mediocrity. The desire to achieve is ingrained in the human heart. People want to advance in their field of endeavor. This is right and good—may I say *normal*? I've never met anyone who wants to fail.

Interestingly, the fear of failure manifests itself in varying kinds of behavior. Some people become paralyzed when they need to make decisions because they fear a step in any direction will be the wrong one. Others seem to be driven forward by their fear: it sets in motion an impetus apart from their own drive or making, a sort of inner thrust. It can produce an almost supernatural power to achieve. Because this drive does not spring from a natural base of thinking, everything seems to get out of proportion.

For example, someone might take a promotion that is justifiably offered but be scared to death she'll be found in time to be an imposter—undeserving of the honor and responsibility. Or the Peter Principle may come into play, and she will accept a position for which she is truly not qualified but which she feels she must accept because declining it would be an indication of failure. Then all she can do is tread water as fast as possible, hoping she won't be discovered. In either case, the going is rough and the anguish is real.

Pauline Clance, a psychologist at Georgia State University,

wrote an interesting book entitled *The Imposter Phenomenon: Overcoming the Fear That Haunts Your Success.* She points out that successful people who suffer from fear of failure often encounter a strange paradox: they keep succeeding. These are people who never feel their success is genuine. Consequently, they always feel the pressing need to prove themselves again.

This feeling is the opposite of low self-esteem. The person with low self-esteem feels unworthy or inadequate to the task and will usually freeze up from fear of failure. But the successful "imposter" keeps on moving right up to the finish line, feeling all the while that she is faking it. These people know they're successful, but they also believe they have gotten where they are only through luck or charm. So they keep redefining success. "When they get a success, they raise the definition of real success another rung on the ladder," Clance says. "If they've done one good movie, next time they need to do a bigger, better movie. And the next time, if they don't win an Oscar, it's obvious to themselves that they're just fakes after all."[1]

Fear of failure drives us into very interesting alternate routes, doesn't it? Danuta Soderman, former co-host of *The 700 Club*, probably the most widely watched program in Christian television, tells of how she overcame this malady. At the age of seventeen, she confessed, she was extremely shy. Living in Alaska with her mother after her parents' divorce, she became deeply confused and had no confidence in herself. She was certain she would never amount to anything in life.

Her mother found an ad in the newspaper for the Miss Anchorage Beauty Pageant. She asked Danuta, "Why don't you enter this?"

"I can't do that!" Danuta said. "I can't stand up there in

front of everybody and act like I'm perfect. People will look at me, and they'll know I'm not perfect."

Her mother replied, "All you have to do is walk on that stage and act like you own the joint. And nobody will know that you don't."[2]

Those six words, "Act like you own the joint," made a lasting impression on Danuta Soderman. She entered the contest, and every time she got scared she remembered that line. She not only won the talent division, but also got second runner-up in the contest. She says that from that moment on she knew other people saw value in her, so she stopped feeling she had to be perfect. "Waking up to that was the beginning of the beginning for me," she said.[3]

Oh my! The times I have feared failure—I've lost count. I recall the day I became a manager in Mobil Oil Corporation's West Coast Pipelines Department. I was scared to death. Offered the promotion, I vacillated between accepting and rejecting it. *Can I do it? What if I don't know enough? I'm not qualified. I'll make too many mistakes.* On and on my reasoning went, filling me with questions and self-doubts. This was a bigger job than I had ever held in my life, with greater responsibilities and greater chances for bombing on a massive scale.

I remember talking with a close friend in the Dallas Mobil office at that time. Martha Daniel is retired now, but then she was serving as a coordinator in the employee relations department and personally knew many executives in the corporation. I voiced my fears and concerns to Martha, never realizing her input would be as valuable to me as it was. More than anything, I think I was seeking sanctuary for my troubled spirit rather than an answer to my concern.

Nevertheless, Martha listened carefully to all my misgivings and woes, then she said something that I firmly believe was the deciding factor in my accepting the offer. "Of course you can do the job, Luci. I know that for a fact. You'll be perfect for it." She said, "Just remember two things: never sign anything until you're sure, and don't be afraid to ask questions. Everybody on the management level asks questions. That's how things are learned."

Not a single day passes (even now, many, many years later) that I don't think about and use Martha's expert advice. Although given off the cuff, it has helped me immensely. In the same way, "Act like you own the joint" was given with little thought, but it changed a woman's life.

We *need* to hear remarks like that from people we respect, we need to pass them on to others, and we need to remind ourselves of them. *Everybody* is faking it—or thinks she is. Some of us are a little more vulnerable than others, but that's okay. We're stepping out there on faith, moving toward a worthy goal, taking a risk. Trying something—anything—is clearly better than smothering in fear of failure.

At the same time, if we stay among those successful "imposters" who push because they fear failure, we'll never have a place to stop and rest. The cycle will exhaust us, because in order to feel good about ourselves and our profession, we have to keep doing more and more and more. And the result will be burnout.

Early in our professional pursuit, we must learn there's a limit to how much we can sacrifice in pursuit of advancement. Our bodies have natural limits, and we need to heed that rhythm to know when to slow down or absolutely stop.

You know what burnout says to me? It says the individual

who suffers from it is still an amateur, not a professional. It says she took off from the starting gate fueled by bravado, enthusiasm, and expectation but didn't consider the real cost.

An amateur doesn't look ahead. She lives for the first few blocks, not the whole race. And you know what? If she changes jobs, the story will be the same, because burnout doesn't come from an occupation. It comes from the person who has never ordered her priorities nor exercised basic management skills. She may have an executive title, priding herself on accomplishing her job and everyone else's, hanging around her place of business for eighteen hours a day, calling all of this "initiative," but she's never learned to delegate, defer rewards, relegate—in short, use her head.

When burnout occurs, the very best thing one can do is pull over to the side and evaluate. Recognize what she did that caused burnout in the first place. Back off. Let go of the high-powered control reins. Get out into the real world and start developing a private life with family, friends, church, sports, activities. The burned-out woman needs to realize she set her professional sights too low, not too high. When she thought she had arrived, she was actually only beginning. Burnout teaches that lesson—the hard way.

›› ROADBLOCK #2:
Procrastination

Another roadblock that impedes progress almost as much as fear of failure is *procrastination*. The procrastinator has never learned to tell time. It's that basic. Even though procrastinators are preoccupied with time, it remains an enigma to them—as odd as that may sound. They're constantly assessing how much they have left to do and how little time they have to do it in, instead of using that time to get it done.

Procrastinators are interesting people, often very charming, because they spend their whole lives operating and talking in the realm of potentials and possibilities, in a fantasy world of fun and games. They're wishful thinkers, looking for more time than there is on the face of a clock or from dawn to sunset.

The very fact that time is exact, fixed, measurable, and finite is difficult, almost impossible, for the procrastinator to accept. Then, when she is caught short, she's actually surprised or, worse, offended by the clock, herself, or whoever is at hand upon whom she can lay blame.

What makes people procrastinators? Many things. Some don't quite know how to handle a task, so they put it off. Some people feel overwhelmed or dislike what has to be done. Others operate under the eleventh-hour syndrome because it gives them a high. The adrenaline pumps and the mind races, and this adds excitement to an otherwise boring routine. (I have friends who seem to do their best work during the eleventh hour, but for me it would be disaster. I'd feel I was sitting on a time bomb.)

As I said, procrastinators are charming people. But when this habit affects one's work or professional status, it becomes a luxury that cannot be indulged. It blocks one's way to achievement and success.

There has been a lot of information written on procrastination, how to manage one's time, how to get up and get going, and much that's written is excellent and worth applying in our daily lives. I try to use what I've learned and am learning because I, too, am occasionally plagued with voluntary inertia, although I dislike that in myself and fight it tooth and nail.

There are four principles I try to apply to help me around this all-too-common roadblock. Maybe they'll be of benefit to you:

1. Identify the Types of Procrastination Situations

What rings your procrastination bell: An unpleasant task? An overwhelming or complex project? End results being too far away? Solitude? Being afraid of what the results will be? Fear of failure? Feeling stymied?

Whoa! It can be practically anything. Name it for what it is and write it down.

2. Divide the Task into Manageable Parts

This is probably the best principle the procrastinator can learn. Nothing of value is accomplished overnight. Remember that! Everything is a process, and processes take time. Little minutes here and there, put together, create the whole.

This applies when one is losing weight, building a house, writing a book, mastering a sport, saving money, getting an education, rearing children, or learning a language. Whatever it is, start early and work a bit at a time. If need be, chart your course and your progress on paper, but never give up. I didn't say *never stop* or *never have fun* or *never take a break*. I said *never give up.*

If you fear going to the doctor, for instance, because you're concerned about what she'll tell you, start by looking up her number and writing it down. Then have a cup of tea and a time of prayer. Tell the Lord about your fear and anxiety. Ask for His peace and courage. When your prayer is over and your teacup empty, put your hand on the phone and make that call. Stay calm. Keep remembering you've asked for God's courage.

Use it! State your message and ask for an appointment. Prepare daily for that appointment by doing what you can physically, mentally, and spiritually.

When the appointment time comes, go. Try to relax. Call to mind Scriptures you've memorized and believe them! Receive what the doctor tells you like a grown-up, like the mature person you are, and act accordingly.

Maybe the news won't be nearly as bad as you feared. Maybe it'll be worse. But at least you'll know, and your procrastination—in that scene anyway—will be over.

Whatever the task that faces you, start at the beginning and systematically move toward completion. I promise you will complete whatever it is if you simply start and keep moving forward in manageable sections.

3. Don't Ever Wait to Be Prodded

You have a novel idea you think will work? State it. Express yourself. Dr. Margaret Mead's autobiography *Blackberry Winter* features repeated accounts of this unique woman whose new ideas literally forged pioneering achievements in the world of anthropology.

Dr. Mead's father once said to her, "It's a pity you aren't a boy; you'd have gone far." But how much farther could she have gone? This woman who never waited to be prodded liberated herself from convention, living life to the full. She was crowned with awards and medals and honors because she dared unprecedented feats of adventure and saw them to completion, changing the course of anthropological findings forever.

Admittedly, most of us operate on a much smaller scale, but it's the same principle. Don't allow discrimination or tradition to hold you back. We live in a world chock-full of challenges for women. If some challenging undertaking is squelching your professional dream, take the first step and refuse to be wooed by procrastination.

4. Save Some Prime Time for Yourself

Something I learned as a teenager is that I do a lousy job on my hair. I'm just not adept at that skill. Besides, I don't like fooling with it. I dreaded the days I washed my hair because I knew when I finished it still wouldn't please me, no matter how hard I tried. Everything about it pulled my spirit down. Every other day I was low because of this silly, impending obligation I couldn't manage well.

One day it hit me: *This is stupid, Luci. Why go crazy the rest of your life? Have your hair cut short, keep it that way, stop having it colored, and quit this nonsense. Balance your sanity instead of griping all the time.*

So I did. In fact, it's one of the best decisions I ever made, and I'll probably go to my grave with this easy, casual sticky-outy style.

Decide what it is in your life that pulls your spirit down and makes you dread getting up in the morning or coming home at night. Then ask God to help you fix it!

If your house never suits you because it's out of order and you're not a do-it-yourselfer, pay a housekeeper or cleaning person. You'll be amazed how that simple delegation will free your mind and lift your spirit, enabling you to live in surroundings that are straight and clean.

If you don't enjoy cooking, eat more meals out. You don't have to go to the Ritz. Find a good neighborhood restaurant that's not too expensive, and give yourself that luxury. After a while they might even cut you a deal if you keep bringing the whole family!

Have your necessary typing done. Get a baby-sitter for the kids two nights a week. Many of my busy friends even have paid clothes consultants at their beck and call. They phone them, tell them what function needs a new outfit, and the deed is done!

The point is, if you as a busy professional have a tendency to procrastinate because of overwhelming duties unrelated to work, delegate some of those tasks. The change in your spirit will amaze you. Admittedly, you may have to juggle your budget a bit, but take it from one who has the hairstyle to prove it: it's worth every penny. Many things you dread in your private life will take a backseat in your hierarchy of duties and anxieties, and that's very important to your mental health.

For those of you who are procrastinators and have no desire to change, may I suggest you consider joining the Procrastinators Club of America? Their motto is "Time is too valuable to fritter away on essentials." The founder, a Philadelphian named Les Waas, originated the club on a whim in 1956 when he and coworkers joked about "scheduling a meeting for the sole purpose of postponing it." They advertised the never-to-be meeting, drew some responses, and repeatedly canceled it.

The last time I checked, more than four thousand people had joined. Waas speculated that half a million individuals would be members as soon as they got around to it. They all receive a membership card, a License to Procrastinate (ideal for framing), a pin, bumper stickers, and a copy of last month's newsletter. Mr. Waas suggests that those who want to join write for information whenever they find the time: Procrastinators

Club of America, 1111 Broad-Locust Building, Philadelphia, PA 19102. As I said, there are all sorts of ways to maneuver around roadblocks.

>> ROADBLOCK #3:
Transition

The third aspect of life that can clutter the route toward our professional niche is *transition*—change, and all that goes with it.

Over the past thirty years or so, a number of studies have suggested that too many changes—whether controllable or not, positive or negative—can actually make a person sick. To measure this, researchers assigned certain events numerical values and refer to them as "life-change units." Events, such as marriage, changing jobs, losing a job, death of a loved one, birth of a child, excessive debts, divorce, jail terms, moving to a new location, and so on, can be measured in terms of life-change units. The greater the number of these at a particular time, the higher the risk for illness.

What can we do about it? Changes take their toll to different degrees on different people. Some bounce back effectively or even thrive on change, and others fall apart. Why? It seems that those who cope best are the persons with resiliency—the ability to adapt to the aftereffects. In other words, they're the persons who learn to fight change with change; they beat it at its own game. The answer lies in *learning to adjust one's expectation levels* through planning.

What does this mean in practical terms?

If you're planning to move, start getting ready months in advance. Talk with people who've moved; write down the details of what they tell you so you can reflect on them. Be in prayer about your move; ask the Lord to begin the adjustment in your mind and heart immediately. If possible, visit your new home or city. Practice thinking about the positive aspects of the move. Don't dwell on the negatives; commit those to God.

What you're doing is getting rid of a lot of the unknowns. And the reason change can be such a roadblock is that we are going into the unknown, and the unknown is often deeply debilitating.

If you're having surgery, for example, become familiar with what's going to happen. You'll heal faster if you understand more. If you're going to a new job in a company, ask those who've been there what it's like. Read books and articles about people who have served in similar capacities. Expect reality. Instead of imagining the best or the worst prospects, choose the middle. There are trade-offs in everything, and we need to adjust our thinking to accommodate those trade-offs. Unknowns intimidate; therefore, know all you can up-front.

Sometimes, during transition times, it simply helps to focus more intently on our goals. Goals minimize the effects of change because they make us impervious to side effects, and to the goal-setter, change is nothing more than a negative side effect. The dream is out there in the distance. Focusing on it makes us less aware of and less bothered by the changes that are occurring closer to home. We see the dream on the horizon, not the change over by the side of the road.

Change may be a source of irritation, but as Barbra Streisand sings, it won't "rain on our parade." Stand back and view your life objectively from time to time, trying very hard not to blow situations out of proportion. Simply because you're experiencing a life-change unit this month or this year doesn't mean you'll experience it every year until the day you die. God designs these things at certain times in our lives for His own purposes.

One of the signs of a truly Christ-centered professional is the maturity to distinguish between that which will pass and that which will last. On some occasions we must maintain, continue, endure, no matter how much we're criticized, discriminated against, or buffeted. A lot of life is sheer maintenance: simply keeping our spirits vulnerable to God's shaping and honing. Not giving up. Not caving in.

It's our responsibility to learn continuity. But our continuity is tied to a relationship with Christ, not a relationship with this world. Through our commitment to Him and His calling for our lives, He enables us to transcend what would otherwise make us sick, sap our strength, or take away the joy of life.

As Christians we, at times, have the mistaken idea that once we put our lives into God's hands, everything is going to be predictable, stable, and permanent. But this faulty reasoning leads to the delusion that troubles should not come our way.

Then when transitions and problems occur, taking their toll on our spirits and bodies, we wonder what happened, and we often fall apart. We tire of the struggle and our own human frailties. We no longer want to "run with endurance the race that is set before us" (Heb. 12:1). We're sick of the whole debilitating mess and want to throw in the towel, because we're looking for and expecting certainty, not change.

But in this life, certainty is a myth! Here's what we need to remember from Dr. Daniel Taylor: "We do not choose between a life of difficulty and a life of ease. We simply choose *for what purpose* we will work, sometimes suffer, and hopefully endure. I may have more pain than my secular neighbor; I may have less. In either case, my struggles are given an ultimate meaning by the context of a life lived in light of eternity."[4]

That's the key to dealing with change: *always look for an ultimate meaning!* Remember that God is in the business of building our characters, not our empires. Therein lies His purpose for working on us and our purpose for working on ourselves. And therein lies the reason for transition.

> God offers us a person and a relationship; we want rules and a format. He offers us security through risk; we want safety through certainty. He offers us unity and community; we want unanimity and institutions. And it does no good to point fingers because none of us desires too much light. All of us want God to behave Himself in our lives, to touch this area but leave that one alone, to empower us here but let us run things ourselves over there.[5]

This issue of transition is particularly applicable to a large and growing group of women in the professional ranks: working mothers.

With the opening of new opportunities for women in the work force and the resulting exodus from the home, an unfortunate division has developed among women, almost a cold war. And the subject of the war is motherhood.

Too often the traditional mother who believes her place is in the home, rearing her children and finding her means of significance in total integration with family—their routines, problems, and hopes—harbors animosity toward the mother who chooses to work outside the home. The woman who has a career, on the other hand, harbors these same feelings of enmity toward her conventional counterpart.

Who makes the better mother? Battle lines are clearly drawn, and whichever side the mother chooses, she can expect to be criticized and experience reverberations. National organizations support both views, and extremely strong feelings of loyalty boil in both camps.

Let me say at the outset that I'm not a working mother. I am a single, childless, working woman who has observed this war from the sidelines. I don't pretend to be an advocate for either point of view, and the only reason I raise the issue here is that both groups of women are facing a unique transition and dilemma on a daily basis.

This transition is cultural, with no antecedents for guidance. Women do not have the history behind them to know the long-term implications of their choices.

If the traditional mother chooses to stay at home, feeling this is her duty before God, she often has the discomforting thought that had she chosen a profession she might have been a richer person in spirit, a better mother, a more integrated individual into the whole of society. She views her life as being deficient.

By the same token, the mother who reports to the workplace outside her home fights the fear that she's not the mother she should be. Life seems to fall into jagged pieces, fragmented and disquieting because of varied purposes. She views *her* life as being deficient.

Each lifestyle leads to ambivalence about one's own choices. As if these forces of turmoil within were not enough, there is the battle between the two groups of women without. And to resolve the conflict, each mother feels she must justify the correctness of her choice and somehow irrefutably prove this to the opposing side.

No mother has ever verbalized the battle internally and externally better than former Prime Minister Golda Meir, mother of two children herself, who also ultimately came to be known as the mother of modern Israel:

> There are mothers who work only when they are forced to . . . But there is a type of woman who cannot remain home for other reasons. In spite of the place which her children and her family take up in her life, her nature and being demands something more; she cannot divorce herself from a larger social life. She cannot let her children narrow her horizon. And for such a woman, there is no rest . . . this eternal inner division, this double pull, this alternating feeling of unfulfilled duty—today toward her family, the next day toward her work—this is the burden of the working mother.[6]

Research shows that a woman's satisfaction with her role in life makes all the difference in how good she is at parenting, even though she may suffer from frequent inner conflicts. It boils down to how the individual mother feels about herself as a person.

Obviously, Golda Meir had a calling to provide social guidance for a nation, something most mothers do not face. At the outset of her marriage at a young age, she told her husband, Morris, of her dream that Jews must have a land of their own and that she must help to shape it. Reluctantly, he agreed to go to Palestine and live in a kibbutz (a collective farm or settlement in modern Israel).

He hated it. Morris wanted his wife for himself and refused to have children unless they left the kibbutz.

Golda acquiesced. They moved to a tiny apartment in Jerusalem, where their son was born. But still having that pull to play a role in the life of her nation, she felt like a prisoner in her own home. And naturally she hated that.

After the birth of a second child, and bitter resentment because of being prevented from doing the work in Palestine to which she felt called, Golda accepted the defeat of her marriage and returned to work in the movement. She was criticized for being "a public person, not a homebody." Her mother chastised her, as did her sister—the revolutionary who had ignited Golda with the Zionist dream in the first place. Even with all the fine work she accomplished for her country, she constantly suffered from guilt for not having been a "model mother."

The reason I use this story is because it conveys the ongoing dilemma: are working mothers "good" mothers? The fact is this can never be solved by a pat answer that applies to everyone. It *can't* be solved because it's a subjective and relative question. Who can rightfully judge? The nation? The mother's relatives? Or the mother herself? If the story left this question in your mind—*Was Golda as good a mother as she was a national leader?*—then I've proved my point. It's what every working mother faces on a daily basis. And it's okay not to have an answer.

After all, who is a model mother? What does that entail? I know mothers who stay at home for the good of the family as well as themselves, and mothers who work outside the home for exactly the same reasons. Yet there are times when they both wind up doing laundry and grocery shopping in the middle of the night—not because that's motherhood, but because it's life.

As an unmarried woman without children, I do that, too, and it can't be helped. We're each called to many responsibilities that have to be carried out, and to accomplish them we simply have to realize our composure lies in balancing both home and work to the best of our abilities. Modern life can't accommodate all our needs. As women we have to find that equality, that balance within our own hearts and compromises, and we have to work at it all the time.

Good mothers come in all types. The more contented you are with the overall character God is building in your life, the better parent you'll be, and the better professional woman you'll become. My plea is that the war between the employed and the nonemployed mother reach a truce. Accept each other as allies instead of adversaries, and work together to bring about changes that enhance the cause of Christ. Stop quibbling about the arena where you spend the majority of your time. We have much bigger battles to fight as Christian women.

>> ROADBLOCK #4:
Poor Communication

The final roadblock we'd like to circumnavigate is *poor communication*. How we communicate as professional women can frequently make us or break us.

In my mind, successful communication requires two elements that many in the working world neglect: knowing how to talk and knowing how to listen. Sounds simple enough, doesn't it? But it's more difficult than it sounds. In a sense, there's an art to it. Generally, people love to exchange light, easy conversation. They like to laugh and joke and feel relaxed. It's been my experience that employees or colleagues respond more readily and favorably to a supervisor or leader who can make small talk with them. Lee Iacocca once said, "You don't succeed for very long by kicking people around. You've got to know how to talk to them, plain and simple."

That's the secret: plain and simple. Breaking the ice! It can seem on occasion like a waste of time, yet it has the power to open doors to serious discussions and important brainstorming.

Dr. Georgette McGregor, who was a professor of speech before she became a full-time consultant and communications expert, says, "I noticed when I began to work with people who were skilled at big talk that it was something they'd learned how to do. But they really didn't feel at ease with small talk."[7] She points out that while these individuals were successful scientists, specialists, and leaders in big corporations, they generally were not successful at communicating with coworkers and employees.

Casual conversation reflects that you yourself are relaxed and confident about who you are and where you are. You're not standing there wondering what others are thinking of you; you're enjoying what's going on. Small talk is a nonthreatening meeting ground that is effective in leading to deeper exchange of creative ideas, thoughts, and feedback.

Here's our six-word key to managing small talk: *focus in on the other person.* Ask questions. Exhibit genuine interest. Be informal, without a "let's get down to business" attitude. Show that you care about other people as persons, not objects. Once you've done this, it's amazing how much easier it is to accomplish your work.

In her excellent book *Choosing the Amusing,* my dear friend Marilyn Meberg writes:

At work we may spend years with our fellow employees, seeing in them only their success or failures and knowing nothing of their inner life because they are merely objects to us. When they succeed and that success enhances our work environment, we are pleased they have functioned well. When they fail, and that failure inconveniences us, we are irritated.[8]

Right on, Marilyn! That's so true. Too true, unfortunately. But there's hope:

There have been many times when someone ceased to be an object of irritation to me once I heard his or her heart, listened to his or her insecurities, and watched the protective mask slowly lower as I revealed my own insecurities. When I heard that heartbeat in such close synchronization with my own, the person ceased to be an object. That would never have occurred without time and concentration upon our respective persons. Such a focus caused me to understand as well as empathize with what had formerly irritated me. As a result, the person ceased being a performing object and became a valuable person.[9]

The principles Marilyn states are foundationally important to the Christian working woman. Interested in the development of character in both herself and others, she must care about people as persons. Or, as Dr. McGregor states it, she must be "eternally fascinated." Don't miss that double meaning.

Back in the 1980s, *Working Woman* magazine printed a list of the twelve key ingredients of a satisfying job. Listed in the order of their importance, number one was "Interesting and challenging work," and number two was "Management that makes employees feel they are important as individuals."

I'm not saying constructive criticism doesn't have a place, but I *strongly* feel that negative appraisals of employees would be minimized if supervisors simply chatted with people "plain and simple" rather than knocking them dead with a list of their faults. Managers are called to nurture and build, not condemn and destroy. It begins with learning how to chat.

Our last six-word slogan deals with the other side of the communication coin: *try to become an attentive listener.* I have to refer again to *Choosing the Amusing*, because knowing from experience what a superb listener Marilyn is, I can testify that the three suggestions she gives us to be attentive ("empathic," she calls it) really work:

> Listen with your whole body.
> Don't interrupt.
> Enter into the mind and the emotion of the person speaking.[10]

Marilyn encourages us to listen empathetically to others, advising us that this kind of listening mends the spirit as well as lifts the heavy heart.

You're saying, "I don't have time for that stuff. I've got deadlines. I've got a show to run. I don't have the luxury of taking time to zero in on other people, listening and chatting."

But hear me carefully: I'm not advocating that you shut down the shop while everybody sits around all day cracking jokes, drinking coffee, and chatting. I'm advocating that you *care* . . . you care enough to show sympathy, sensitivity, and—dare I say it again?—vulnerability.

Believe me, one of the lovely things about being a feminine professional is that you need not denigrate what comes naturally to you by virtue of being a woman. "What business needs is what women know how to do."[11]

When leadership studies were conducted with the first coed classes at West Point, traditionally a stronghold of masculine values, an interesting fact emerged. While males and females scored equally well on getting the job done, in the evaluations by their subordinates, women rated higher when it came to looking out for subordinates' welfare and showing interest in their lives.

Networking and teamwork should be second nature to women. Most of us are used to picking up signals about people. As we learn to respond positively to those signals, we build communication skills. And that's what true professionalism is all about.

Reflect with me a minute: fear of failure, procrastination, transition, poor communication. Are you unable to get from point A to point B because of one of these roadblocks? Try some of these other ways to get past the barrier:

> Face one day at a time.
> Act like you own the joint.
> Identify the types of procrastination situations.
> Divide the task into manageable parts.
> Don't ever wait to be prodded.
> Save some prime time for yourself.
> Learn to adjust your expectation levels.

> Always look for an ultimate meaning.
> Realize your composure lies in balance.
> Focus in on the other person.
> Try to become an attentive listener.

No more delays. No more potholes or barricades. No more construction equipment blocking your path. No more being out of sorts. You've discovered an alternate route—so start your engine and get moving!

5 the travelers

As women try out new roles and take greater, more visible risks, many are discovering the importance of sharing their experiences with others who have similar concerns. Obviously this kind of cooperation and support doesn't just happen. It takes time, care and commitment to build a network that really works.

—Marilyn Loden
Feminine Leadership

I've always been curious about people—fascinated by them—their fads and fashions, quirks and foibles, hopes and dreams. I like biographies so I can find out what makes people tick, how they think and figure things out, the risks they're willing to take, how they face problems and manage to get through them.

Not only do I enjoy reading about heroes and heroines whose accomplishments leave all of us breathless, but I'm drawn to stories of overcomers—those who fight the odds of abuse, loneliness, addictions, lack of self-respect, or fear of failure to become the leaders we admire today. They work, attend church, carpool the kids, deal with joys and sorrows like the rest of us, but they seem to have something extra: the ability to live ordinary lives in extraordinary ways. I believe their secret lies in the attitude they maintain about life, one made of faith, humor, courage, and purpose. They've learned how to juggle lots of balls in the air while keeping both feet on the ground and not toppling over when a strong wind blows.

In this chapter I'll introduce you to five women who fall into this category. They come from different backgrounds and their careers have taken them down unique paths, but they all embody the kind of balance and passion this book is about. Each is a Christian, an encourager, a care-taker, and a dear friend. I count it an honor to know them personally and spend time with them.

Being interested in the roads they traveled to arrive at their desired goals, I interviewed these women with specific questions in mind. Although their answers varied somewhat, there's a common denominator threaded throughout every interview: their genuine love for people and desire to help others any way they can. This bond was what put them over the top for me in terms of wanting to share with you their courage, tenacity, strength, and compassion.

As you read the interviews, please keep in mind that all five women have experienced the same fears and needs you and I have—money problems, time constraints, demands from family and friends, and their own personal demons. Yet with faith and common sense they've kept going, trusting God to help them fulfill each task as it came up. Perhaps their vulnerability and achievements will be an encouragement to you as well. They certainly are to me!

Now you can be a little mouse in the corner as you get to know these wonderful women. Take their words of wisdom with you for your own journey ahead.

›› EXAMPLE #1:
Andrea Grossman

Since 1979 we've been using papers, stickers, and creative tools from Mrs. Grossman's Paper Company to make life more fun. Our teacher and friend, even when we didn't know it, was Andrea Grossman, the founder and president of this unique enterprise. This deeply loved graphic artist, whose hallmark is always quality and good taste, has also written a book that was published in 2004, *Designer Scrapbooks with Mrs. Grossman*. It's full of her artwork, scrapbooks, photos, and ideas.

Andrea has been featured in *People* magazine, the *New York Times*, and *USA Today*. But the most noteworthy and endearing thing about this generous woman is her love for the Lord and dedication to helping people. A few months ago, we talked about her work, beliefs, and challenges.

LUCI: *Do you think being a Christian makes you a better business owner?*

ANDREA: That depends on what kind of Christian you are, I guess. But I would answer that emphatically yes. Being a firm believer gives you groundwork to measure your decisions against, and your values and vision against.

LUCI: *Do you do that daily?*

ANDREA: Absolutely.

LUCI: *Can you give me an example?*

ANDREA: On the way to work I drive through beautiful countryside, and I just feel overwhelmed with the need to commit the company to the Lord: "This is Your company, Lord. You brought it into existence, and once again I commit it to You and ask that You guide me in every decision I make today and the way I treat people." It's different every day; I say whatever comes to mind.

LUCI: *How did you get started?*

ANDREA: I was a graphic designer, and as a mother and wife I felt I had to do something to help our income, but I didn't want to work full-time. My husband was an oil painter. So I prayed about it, asking the Lord to guide me in a company that would (1) express my talents, (2) help my family, and (3) uplift and have meaning for other people.

LUCI: *Do you feel God has answered those requests?*

ANDREA: Oh, absolutely! I see things He does that are just miraculous in this company—things beyond my understanding. He gives me bumps along the way too. Sometimes you fall into a ditch and have to pull yourself out, with His help.

LUCI: *When you review these things as a business owner who wants to honor the Lord, does it make you glad you've focused on uplifting others—and would you do it again if you had to?*

ANDREA: Yes. I never left that position, ever. The foundational building block was that I wanted to help my family. Oddly enough it did, even though there was a divorce involved. God has used my talents, as mediocre as they are. And He has uplifted people.

This last Sunday was Easter, for example, and we were interviewed on a Sunday morning show. When I checked my e-mail the next day, there were at least eight letters from people who said they saw the show and what a good job we're doing: "I'm so glad you're doing this for other people, and I'm going to buy more stickers than I ever have." God shows His hand.

LUCI: *As a Christian entrepreneur, do you think ambition plays a part?*

ANDREA: I think ambition has sort of a negative meaning, but it certainly plays a part because you couldn't be an entrepreneur without it. Call it "stick-to-it-iveness" or "focus" or "determination" or "stamina." It's important because starting a business, running it, dealing with people, hiring, disciplining, encouraging is a lot of work. Whether it's ambition or a strong conviction, you need it.

LUCI: *Do you ever wish you weren't the boss?*

ANDREA: I love my business for all the reasons I've discussed: the people, the customers, the kind of products we make. And I feel it's a really good, healthy business. But there are times it's hard to get up and go to work. Do I ever wish I weren't the owner? Yeah, I do. Not often, but there are times I wish I could shove this mantle off my back. But I know I'd be a lousy employee, so . . .

LUCI: *When you're the boss, you have to fire people, handle things that are painful. That's hard for a caring person, and for a believer.*

ANDREA: If you don't get a good stomachache when you have to fire somebody, you're not much of a person. You're dealing with people's lives, and you can never forget that. I realized way into my business that people are afraid of losing their jobs. I never would have thought that because I'm not fearful, but they really are. So, that's always a weight on your shoulders. Another thing might be dealing with a big account that's difficult. You might not even like the customer, but you have to deal with him or her. But I have to say also that being the boss gives you an opportunity to grow a whole lot faster than being an employee does.

LUCI: *Which is more important to you: being fulfilled as a person or knowing the work your employees are doing is fulfilling to them?*

ANDREA: I think if I focus on what my employees are getting out of the job, it makes me more fulfilled as a person.

LUCI: *One is sort of predicated on the other, isn't it? If you're making other people happy by your own generosity, it makes you happy as well.*

ANDREA: Yes. You always want to pull them up, give them opportunities to do better—which is really fun, to watch people grow. That's my favorite thing. And I've seen a lot of that happen.

LUCI: *How do you account for your tremendous success in a very competitive market?*

ANDREA: That's an easy answer: because we worked very hard at the beginning. We built a good reputation with our customers, our sales reps, and our vendors. There's lots of competition now in that we have to be extremely innovative to offer new, refreshing stickers.

LUCI: *Are people drawn to the new?*

ANDREA: Oh yes. Stickers used to last fifteen years—five years minimum. Now they last six to twelve months. You can't predict anything. The market is just outrageous.

LUCI: *Which do you think is harder to keep in balance: motherhood or a successful business?*

ANDREA: I think motherhood is harder. My forty-year-old son works for me. He'll be running it someday. I hand things off to him gradually. So that little difference between being a partner and being a mother is something I always have to keep in balance. I often want to mother him, correct him, and yet I have to constantly get out of that role and be his employer/partner. I don't think success is that hard to keep in balance because everything I am and have I owe to the Lord anyway.

LUCI: *If you could have more time, energy, or money, which would you choose?*

ANDREA: Time. There are so many things I want to do. I guess because the company's been so good to me, I want to share that and let more people do the same kind of thing. And I just don't have enough time for it.

LUCI: *You're so organized, I would think that alone would give you more time. What's your secret for organization?*

ANDREA: I have so many components in my life, I have a hard time keeping them straight, actually. Papers that come across my desk, for example, letters, donations, schedules, financials—there's a flood that comes in every day. Because I'm not really interested in all that, I prioritize what needs to be done first, and what can be, I push back. I'm a color organizer. Even my closet is done in color.

LUCI: *I love that. You mean if swimsuits and ball gowns are both red, they hang together?*

ANDREA: Yes. Everything is color-coded, all my files and every task I do. In fact, I've been able to compartmentalize my life into six colors. Design is red; sales, orange; marketing, pink; export (this includes travel in my case), blue; personal things, purple; financial, green; administration—anything to do with legal or company policies—yellow. It's very helpful. I'd just say to organize your life, divide the components and color them. Believe it or not, it helps.

LUCI: *What helps is to be an artist!*

ANDREA: Yes, being an artist affects the way I look at everything. I'm aware of the colors of every day. I take these little photographs all the time, making little visual decisions. It enriches one's whole life. And graphic design is a wonderful field, always changing. Because I'm an artist, I probably would have always chosen this profession.

LUCI: *What's the best advice an employer can give an employee?*

ANDREA: A lot of different things—I don't know that there's a "best." But when I hire somebody, I always explain that we're a team and we support one another. I encourage them to think about who they're working with more than their own agenda, and to do the very best work they can within the confines of where the company is and what the company's mission is. Honesty is so important, even when things aren't going well. Don't try to hide things or push them under the carpet.

Luci: Are you a confronter?

Andrea: No, I don't enjoy it. It's possible to confront decently, but it depends, of course, on what you're confronting. If it's someone who's rude, that's different from confronting someone who's wrong about something.

Luci: Do you think every company should have a mission statement?

Andrea: Definitely. And every person should have one. It helps you know where you're going, and you have a framework to work within. When I started my company, I sat down and made myself tell myself why I wanted to do this. I think if you start something and you aren't honest with yourself about why you're doing it, you're going to be flailing around a lot. It just gives you a foundation and a benchmark.

Luci: Do you feel your mission statement could ever become out-of-date or archaic?

Andrea: No, because it's based on timeless operating principles. J. P. Edwards, the software firm, has a mission statement that simply says, "To honor God." Why would you want to change that? And again, it's a little measurement: are we honoring God with this, or are we just trying to make more money? Are we taking advantage of other people? If you have a mission statement, I think it keeps you in check as well as moving you forward and keeping you focused.

LUCI: Have you ever faced a situation where the going was really tough and you had to take some hard risks?

ANDREA: Yes, and those were some of my best times. I don't mind taking a risk. Early in our career, the company went from a skyrocket to a bomb. I prayed a lot because my divorce was happening, the company was in distress, we owed a lot of money, and I determined I was not going out of business in debt (a couple million dollars at that time). Also, I didn't want to walk away from what I had started. So I stayed in constant contact with the Lord, and He gave me the strength to keep going and the skill to do things I didn't know how to do, such as read a financial statement, negotiate with my vendors to allow me some leeway, work with the bank to which I owed a lot of money. The Lord gave me incredible ability to learn more, to keep going, and to make good decisions.

LUCI: Did these hard times serve you well in the long run? Did they make you a better leader?

ANDREA: Oh yes. I'm uncomfortable when we're on a high because number one, I know there's going to be a change, and number two, I don't know if we're geared up for it. I don't like highs as well. When you have to pull out every resource to go through something, it's a lot more exciting than just riding on a board on a good wave. When you're walking by faith, you're more careful about what risks you take.

LUCI: How much do you trust your intuition?

ANDREA: A lot. But it's intuition that's based on the foundation of experience. What keeps you from getting in a car with kids who have been drinking? It's not just that your mother told you never to do that, because my mother never told me not to do that. I just knew it. Intuition.

LUCI: *As you know, I love the great hymns of the faith. The words are encouraging and thought-provoking, and I know you feel the same. For example, when you think of "When I Survey the Wondrous Cross," what do those words mean to your deepest heart: "When I survey the wondrous cross, on which the Prince of Glory died, my richest gain I count but loss, and pour contempt on all my pride"?*

ANDREA: When you take time to go to the cross, it puts everything else in a pretty shallow perspective. Nothing else matters very much. If that song doesn't make you realize you're just a servant of His, I don't know what will. It causes you to live your life to honor Him and delight Him. He has spared me from so many things and given me the most wonderful, blessed life. I owe it all to Him.

LUCI: *What is your best definition of a well-lived life? Do you have one?*

ANDREA: I guess my short definition, off the top of my head, would be, Have you used your life well in the service of others and for the Lord? If you can answer yes to that, that would be a well-lived life. I think my life is getting there. It entails some sacrifices. When I was a young person, I would never have thought of hugging these kids at Hunter's Point (an area where so many underprivileged children live) and loving them and encouraging them, or working with people with disabilities. But now that's what I love the most.

At our next outreach, we need a lot of people to duplicate artwork, samples of our sticker art, so we're going to look through Joni & Friends to people in wheelchairs who can do it. We want to help other people all we can.

The bottom line is, I believe God blesses us so we can bless others. Doing that is one of the greatest joys of my life.

›› EXAMPLE #2:
Anne Lamott

Bingo! The first book I read by Anne Lamott was *Bird by Bird* (a book about writing, among other things). I hit the jackpot. She made me laugh and cry, think and feel. I loved everything about this woman: her stream of consciousness, use of imagery, her mind, honesty, freedom. I simply couldn't get enough. Eventually, I located everything she wrote and set about reading it. Little did I know several years later I'd not only meet her, but we'd become friends.

Annie is fall-over funny. She can take the poorest setting in the world and turn it into pure gold, the most inane things of life and give them back wrapped in humor and pathos. Not only that, but she's probably one of the richest proponents of grace in today's Christian culture because of her own incredible story of redemption. Author of both fiction and nonfiction, Anne Lamott writes things that are a mirror image of ourselves in both the human condition and the change that comes when that condition is transformed by Jesus Christ.

> LUCI: *I love your writing. Did you always have aspirations to write—even as a child, did you write little pieces or keep a journal?*

> ANNE: I always wrote. But no, I never kept a journal and I don't now. One thing you and I probably have in common is that I always loved to read. From about four years old on, I always had a book in my hand. I love storytellers and what storytelling does to our hearts and our spirits. It turned out I had a gift for that, so I was just sort of off and running. I could make people laugh, for one thing. I wrote a lot of poems and my father was a writer, so I started out writing stuff to please him.

> LUCI: *I was thinking your father was a professor.*

> ANNE: No, he was a writer—Kenneth Lamott. He also taught English to the inmates at San Quentin and wrote a book called *Chronicles of San Quentin* that was published in *The New Yorker*. He wrote four novels and four works of nonfiction.

> LUCI: *What is the first thing you remember writing?*

ANNE: I remember two things. One was my father wrote me a postcard from Seattle with a snowy owl on it. Isn't that funny, because I get in the shower with my glasses on. I can't remember to turn the car off when I'm going to the market. But I can remember a postcard I got forty-some years ago. It said, "Dear Annie, I would love it if you would write me a story about this owl." So I wrote him a one-page story with my neat little script about this snowy owl.

In the second grade I wrote two poems. One won a California State Teachers award, and one was about John Glenn that went, "Colonel John Glenn went up to heaven in his spaceship *Friendship Seven* . . ." There were like four hundred other verses, all in that same kind of rhyme. I won some awards. I got like gold stars and stickers on them so—yeah! I just always wrote. It always came easily to me.

LUCI: *Do you still love it as you once did?*

ANNE: I love to write right now, I can say. I go through periods where I find it pretty hard going. I don't find it so natural anymore. I get sick of the sound of my own voice. And sometimes I think I'm just beating a dead horse. But right now, even as we speak almost, I'm writing a fifty-page triptych that will serve as an introduction to a second selection of pieces like *Traveling Mercies*—pieces on spirituality and faith.

LUCI: *You used to teach writing courses. Would you rather teach or learn? Which is more gratifying?*

ANNE: I love not teaching, actually. I realized this about five years ago when I was teaching at a big bookstore. Forty people brought in their work every week. I liked it, but it took a tremendous amount out of me. It left me kind of exhausted the next day, which took out a day a week of my writing time. I finally felt like everything I know about writing had been said somewhere or the other. I felt I had communicated what experience, strength, and hope I had.

But I love to learn. I'm always, always learning. I love to be at home. Almost every day I find something I'm absolutely fixated about for no particular reason. Like, the other day I suddenly wanted to immerse myself in Alger Hiss and Whitaker Chambers—isn't that funny?

I went on-line and printed out some really great educational stuff from different universities. Often I'll just immerse myself in someone. Or Sam will have something due from school and I'll help him look it up, and that'll be a really fun way to learn. And you know what? I always loved to learn. I was one of those freaks that loved school. Always.

LUCI: *I did too. I even loved homework.*

ANNE: I didn't mind homework at all. I *loved* it. I just always wanted to read. I had this great thirst. I had a father who really facilitated that, who would hand me books and get me talking about certain things. I remember he'd give me "Prufrock," you know, and we'd read and read. I was pretty young to be reading "Prufrock."

LUCI: *The poem by T. S. Eliot, "The Love Song of J. Alfred Prufrock"?*

ANNE: Yeah, I'd be reading T. S. Eliot at maybe fourteen and he'd say, "Who does that mean: 'Let us go now'? Who's 'us'? Who's he talking to?" I had a real stimulation to understand things more.

LUCI: *Tell me about your lectures.*

ANNE: I lecture once a month, and I usually do one benefit a month too. Of everything I do, I love benefits most of all. I don't mind not being paid because I do well in the other realms of writing or lecturing. What I love most about benefits is that's where I most feel I'm doing God's work. It's kind of missionary work where I can help raise money for the needy or for people who want to have a better future, for their kids, for their community, or for women with breast cancer. That's what I love; it's where I'm happiest.

LUCI: *When you're writing, how do characters in a novel come to you? Are they in your head already, or do they morph out of the plot?*

ANNE: I usually have the idea for a character—that's where the novel starts. One will come to me, like Mattie in *Blue Shoe*, or Rosie, who came fully formed twenty-plus years ago. I can just see them, and I start there. Little by little, they reveal more to me.

LUCI: *What makes a good author?*

ANNE: The authors I love are a really reliable narrator for me in some piece of the world, or some way of living, or some geographic location that I'm interested in. What they're saying is really true, and I'm grateful for somebody relaying that information to me. And if somebody can make me laugh, I'm so *in*. I'll pay extra—I'll kill for a sense of humor.

I also love stuff that I recognize as really being human life as I've understood it, but at the same time, that throws on the lights for me so that I kind of know it for the first time.

LUCI: *Would you rather write fiction or nonfiction?*

ANNE: Nonfiction is a lot easier, I think, for obvious reasons. Mostly, it has happened. Writing nonfiction is more like being a journalist. But I have to say I've always loved fiction. I've always loved novels. And there's a certain way in which I think people can tell a deeper truth in fiction than in nonfiction; it's like eating lasagna—five or six layers come together in each bite. With a novel you can have each character, the time, setting, location, theme, all the sensual information— the smells, what people are hearing, what they look like—all of it in each bite. I love that. But it takes a lot more stamina to write a novel. It takes about three years, so I have to really be geared up for it.

Whereas with nonfiction I could write about our visit today and make it useful to people. I used to tell

my students in lectures to write about what they love
to come upon because it's usually information from
deep inside their souls and it resonates with them. Like
Operating Instructions. When I wrote that, there were
no books on what it's really like that first year with a
little kid. They were all sort of candy-coated. So I
thought I'd love it if a mother, who's stressed out and
exhausted and a little ambivalent, would just tell the
truth. I thought I'd love to have it be, you know, philo-
sophical and practical but also really funny. And so that
really guides me. I write what I'd love to come upon.

LUCI: *Is it hard to balance motherhood with book deadlines?*

ANNE: Without sounding self-aggrandizing, I think being
a mother and being a writer are two of the hardest
things we do. It's *crazy* being a mother, and it's hard
enough just to write. But in both cases they're choices
I decided to undertake. Both of them have great blessings for me, and they're who I am and what I do in the
world. But either is a full-time job.

I feel like it's taken me to the age of fifty to really
find balance in my life. One of the things about getting
older is how much stuff you no longer agree to do.
When I was thirty or forty, I would just say, "Aw, I'll
try to do that" or "I'll help you with that" because I
wanted people to love me. But now I say no to almost
everything. No is a complete sentence! And in order to
be an okay mom and an okay writer, I say no to almost
everything so that I can work all day and take my tiny

nap and a shower, then get to have the afternoon to play out however I want to. It's free choice, you know.

LUCI: *What would you like your writing to do for people in the long run?*

ANNE: I want to give people hope. I think the world has gotten so terrifying; it's so dark and scary. I would really love to say I know what it feels like to be scared and nuts: this is the last time I went through it, and this is what happened. I just love to make people laugh and to give them hope.

LUCI: *Laughter's great medicine for hopelessness.*

ANNE: I think nothing gives hope like laughter because it means the hardness is broken—the hardness of your heart and the armor that you have up because you're feeling so afraid. When someone can make you laugh, it's so moisturizing to your soul.

LUCI: *Is writing a calling or a profession?*

ANNE: Although it's both, I feel I have a calling, and I feel it most when I'm lecturing. I'm in my element to just be talking. Talking comes more naturally to me than anything on earth. And I feel really called to be a hope-giver, a hope-keeper.

LUCI: *Which is harder, Annie, being a Christian author or a secular author?*

ANNE: I think it's embarrassing to be a Christian writer.

LUCI: *That's hilarious!*

ANNE: It's about as unhip as you can possibly get. I mean, you meet these perfectly brilliant, cool people, and they can't believe you're a Christian because they're hip-slickin' cool and very, very intellectual and you're this nice, Jesus-y person, and they're kind of horrified. And if you want to keep them, you have to kind of convince them you're a Christian writer but you have a really open mind and a great thirst for knowledge— that you don't buy into a really narrow, fundamentalist sense of the world. You're open to all of life even if it doesn't jive with what you wish were true—you know, you're just reporting it and working with it.

LUCI: *Do you ever think you'd give up Jesus to be more hip?*

ANNE: Well, Jesus is the only thing I really ultimately have, so no, I couldn't give up Jesus. It would be like giving up an organ or something. Maybe I could conceivably be kept alive for a while, but that which gives me real life would have been taken away and I would probably die. I just would. Jesus is my breath, and without Jesus the despair would be annihilating to me.

LUCI: *Are most of your followers believers?*

ANNE: No. I would say most are seekers. They're searching for something—they're in limbo. Many have felt they were run out of their homes when they were little or teenagers because their parents were very, very strict Christians. So they ran for their lives when they were old enough to. They ran for the world or college or work or for their own authentic spirituality. And somehow they started to get this tug on the sleeve from Jesus. They heard that Jesus is here and clearing His throat and available.

And a lot of people aren't believers at all. They just like my writing.

LUCI: *Annie, do you think you'll ever get married? I know you're dating a really, really wonderful guy. Do you think you'll marry him?*

ANNE: I could marry, but no, I don't think I will because I no longer think marriage is the prescription for happiness. I think your daily conscious contact with God is your only hope. You know, I used to think if you were just really thin and had long legs, you'd be fine. And then I found a lot of people who did fit in and were beautiful, "normal" people. They had money, got married to good-looking guys, had kids and nice houses, yet were all in the same boat: what they wanted wasn't out there.

My experience has been that there are very, very few happily married people. And now I just thank the Lord for my freedom and that I didn't have a bad marriage—that He let me flail and flounder. But there's a part of me this side of the grave that will always think if you're really thin and have long legs, you're fine.

LUCI: *I know you love the hymn "What a Friend We Have in Jesus." What do the words mean to you personally?*

ANNE: That hymn means everything to me personally. It's funny; I've been talking about this lately: everything I know about Jesus that's important can be captured in the songs we sing to our three- to five-year-olds. You know, "Jesus Loves Me," "Jesus Loves the Little Children"—these are the things about Jesus we know for sure. And "What a Friend We Have in Jesus" is the same way because I don't have esoteric thoughts on Christianity; I don't have brilliant insight into Scripture or the Bible as a whole; but I know I have a friend in Jesus, and I talk to Him all the time. He's like my older, slightly hippie brother.

Wherever I am, I'm in Jesus, and He's in me, and I can breathe again. The Holy Spirit is filling my spiritual lungs and oxygenating my brain. I remember who I am and whose I am and that as Jesus's younger sister, I'm covered. So yeah, "What a Friend We Have in Jesus" is my favorite hymn.

LUCI: *What is your best definition of a well-lived life? Do you have one?*

ANNE: A well-lived life is like having created a garden with all the weeds and brambles and roots and bugs and grubs. It's when you think you wouldn't have traded any of your life for the world because all the pain and mess became compost. The Holy Spirit made it become this really fertile soil in which things grew and kept surprising you and feeding you. It's the joy of the dreck turning into beauty.

Sometimes you've just given up all hope because it's cold and rainy and it sucks, but you need it all. Then the bulbs—narcissus, daffodils, and tulips—come up and they make such a great resurrection every year. Resurrection is a wonderful thing.

>> EXAMPLE #3:
Mary Graham

As guardian of Women of Faith's highest calling, Mary Graham brings a collection of gifts to the presidency of this organization that encourages and blesses all of us every day. She's compassionate, gracious, intuitive, wise, and extremely conscientious. Not only that, but her razor-sharp wit has softened and refocused many difficult situations. Who wouldn't want these attributes in a leader and a friend?

Serving three decades with Campus Crusade for Christ, Mary traveled to the four corners of the earth, taking the same message of hope and joy to everyone she met. She's faced numerous challenges, and because of her quick mind and innate kindness, Mary knew how to resolve them. I asked for this interview to give you a peek at some of her common-sense insights about life and work.

LUCI: *Have you always been intuitive? Were you like this as a child, or did you acquire intuition as you went along?*

MARY: I think it's the way I was wired from the womb. And since then, it's been important, intentional. I've leaned on my intuition a lot. I force myself to trust the data. I hate it when the data proves me wrong, but of course it does sometimes. When you're dealing with people and ideas, intuition serves you really well, but when you make a very strategic decision, you'd better have backup.

LUCI: *For many years you were in ministry with Campus Crusade for Christ. Do you think that prepared you for what you do today?*

MARY: One hundred percent! I had no idea the road I traveled would bring me to this place. I've had experience through the years trusting God and operating out of a sense of mission, focusing on a very strong purpose. I've been mentored by people with a sense of mission.

LUCI: *What's your favorite thing about being president of Women of Faith?*

MARY: I really love what we're doing as an organization. I can think of fifty jobs in Women of Faith I'd be very content doing because I love the end result in the lives of the audience, the staff, the speakers, the production team. I mean, we're all growing and having a great time doing it. That's what happens when people come to the conference.

LUCI: *Do you have a least favorite?*

MARY: My least favorite is the fear factor. What if I do the wrong thing? It would kill me if we held back in an area where we should be expansive, and it would embarrass me if we expanded in an area and failed. The good news is I don't make those decisions by myself. We operate very much as a team, so there's no decision that's mine alone. But I do feel a sense of responsibility, and the buck stops with me. I don't want to make a mistake.

LUCI: *Would you say you're a risktaker?*

MARY: No. I don't like risks. Risks lead to trouble and criticism and getting your feelings hurt, and those are my three least favorite things in life.

LUCI: *Yeah, but risky people get things done. They're pioneers. How do you manage to stay on the cutting edge and not take risks?*

MARY: I take risks every day, but I live in complete denial about that. I think about wanting to help; that's the reason I came to Women of Faith in the first place. I wanted to help. I saw a need and wanted to meet it. That's my total motivation for everything. I mean, if I saw a baby on the street with a wet diaper, I'd stop and change it. And so to be the one who is helping—to be in that position—is what I want. John 20:3 refers to Peter and "the other disciple"; I would much rather be "the other disciple." I don't want to be the one whose name everybody knows. I like being right there in the middle of things, but I don't necessarily want anybody to know who I am.

LUCI: *How do you view your place in the working world: is it a profession or a calling?*

MARY: It's completely a calling. But knowing me, it would be a calling if I worked at Starbucks. I think of all the people who need something to drink and I could give them the perfect thing . . . a word of cheer or something with their coffee could help them. Life is a mission, and I'm on it.

LUCI: *Do you have a hard time enjoying leisure?*

MARY: Leisure is not part of my mission. I want to help somebody else, and it's hard for me at times to take care of myself. Even if I'm on hold on the phone, I can never just relax. I have to be sending an e-mail or writing a letter or something. That's why I'm always spilling something. Even when I go on vacation, it's hard for me to do nothing.

LUCI: *I'm glad it's your calling, Mary. We're all the richer for it because you're a wonderful leader. What do you think makes a good leader?*

MARY: The most important thing is that you have to really care about people. A good leader has to have a lot of compassion and empathy. You also have to have tremendous clarity about where you're going and how you're going to get there. I call it a "north star"—you set your sight on it and all roads have to go in that direction. We can't go in fifteen different directions at a time. Focus is *everything* in leadership.

We have a very clear mission statement, vision, and purpose, and we measure decisions against it. I think it's very caring for a leader to do that. To me, nothing is more frustrating in a boss (and I've had 'em) than one day thinking *this* is important and the next day thinking something else. It's maddening. You think, *We're never going to get anything done* because all you do is go in circles.

LUCI: *Do you think there are people in Christian work who aren't good leaders?*

MARY: Of course. They're in every organization, politics, business. They don't care about people, are dishonest, and have no character. Then there are people who are very good administrators; they get a lot of work done and can manage huge tasks, but they are not good at leading.

LUCI: *Is it harder to find the person who's right for the job or to fire the person who's wrong for the job?*

MARY: I find both extremely difficult. One of the hardest things in my life is to fire somebody. It takes me forever. In fact, I once fired a person three times in one year; I just couldn't bring myself to make her walk out the door. It's very hard to fire someone, and almost impossible to fire someone well.

Finding the right person for the job is also hard, especially in an organization like Women of Faith because there's so much enthusiasm that surrounds what we're doing. It's very exciting, and a lot of people want to be a part of that.

LUCI: *In the hymn "Trust and Obey," the first verse starts with these words: "When we walk with the Lord / In the light of His Word / What a glory He sheds on our way." What do you think that means?*

MARY: Those words mean God illumines the path I'm on because I'm walking with Him. I'm no longer in the dark. He gives not only direction but blessing. It's when you know what to do and you have no idea how you know it, but you can't get the smile off your face.

LUCI: *And that's not intuition, is it? It's from walking and trusting and obeying?*

MARY: Right. And for me it feels like it takes my breath away a little bit . . . like *aha*. When I sense that, it's like I know exactly what to do, almost as if it comes in a flash. But I've walked with the Lord so long I recognize it.

LUCI: *How long have you been a Christian?*

MARY: I really understood how to put my faith in Christ when I was a junior in college—that was thirty-eight years ago. And in all that time I've worked in ministry. I always wanted to do for others what somebody did for me: helping me understand how to have a personal relationship with God, trusting Him for everything.

And I can think of many times when God shed

His glory on my way. It's very exciting because people ask me, "Oh, how did you do this or that?" or "Do you consider yourself responsible for the success of Women of Faith?" and I think, *No.* I'm just grateful that the Lord has kept me walking with Him. His Spirit illumines my reality.

You know, I saw Him, I responded to Him, I hung on to Him, and I've been hanging on to Him for dear life ever since. In many ways I am very insecure. So I believe faith has been easier for me than a person who is extremely self-sufficient. I don't know, never having been self-sufficient. And when God shows up, I think, *Who would want to live any other way?*

LUCI: *What's the greatest tool for advancing in the work-place: education, knowledge of Scripture, walking with the Lord, being in the right place at the right time?*

MARY: All of the above. And I would never underestimate natural ability.

LUCI: *You mean intelligence and talent?*

MARY: Yes, giftedness—that's very important. But I wouldn't underestimate education either. The more you learn, the broader you are, the better you are at doing any kind of job. I believe that if you walk with God, He equips you and enables you to do the impossible and be all He's created you to be.

LUCI: *Have you ever wanted to throw in the towel?*

MARY: Yes, many times I want to quit, but it usually has to do with something outside myself—if I get my feelings hurt or my spirit gets quenched because a person criticizes me or doesn't understand. That's very hard for me. I don't often want to quit from feeling overwhelmed or being frustrated by work.

LUCI: *How do you get your equilibrium back?*

MARY: I have to get God's perspective, and I can do that in one of two ways. One, I go to my trusted counselors, who remind me that I'm not an idiot or total failure. Two, I go to the Lord, who reminds me of what His Word teaches and He lifts my spirit. Fortunately, it doesn't last long.

LUCI: *Does it help to have a sense of humor?*

MARY: Oh yes. I remember one time when we had this horrible, massive snafu. It had to be solved immediately, and we had to work through it very carefully. I called my vice president, and when we connected, we laughed our heads off at the absurdity of it all: just the incongruity of "How could this have happened?" mixed with "Only God can figure this out." It wasn't nearly as fearful after that. And then we solved it.

LUCI: *Not long ago in church, we were singing the hymn "Blessed Assurance." You told me you loved the words: "Blessed assurance, Jesus is mine. / Oh, what a foretaste of glory divine!" Why do you like that?*

MARY: Because assurance means everything to me. I grew up in a church where I was not well taught. It never crossed my mind I could know anything for sure: if I was behaving enough to please God; if I would go to heaven when I died; if God heard my prayers, much less answered them; if life was dependent on my behavior or what kind of mood God was in. I grew up in a home where there was a lot of emotional disarray. So you could never be sure when you came home if things were going to be peaceful or chaotic.

LUCI: *Wasn't that scary?*

MARY: It was very scary. My mother's personality was very consistent, but my dad's was not. I never knew what was going to upset him. I was always on guard. And I guess because of the way I interpreted that (at least with the little I knew about God), I wondered what was going to make Him mad next. And how mad would God get?

LUCI: *Were you afraid of your father?*

MARY: Yes, very afraid, and I equated that with God having the upper hand. So in a way it was very important in my development as a person because I learned to be very high functioning. I'm not sure I would have if I hadn't been so challenged in my childhood. My dad always found something else he wanted us to prove. He believed if he ever told us we did well, we'd stop trying to do better. And if he told us we couldn't do it, we'd prove we could.

So assurance to me is *so* blessed. I hear myself pray every day, "Thank You, Lord, that You love me, thank You that I belong to You, and thank You that You're there." Even when I confess my sin, I know God doesn't move away from me because I've offended Him. Nothing is more blessed to me than assurance.

LUCI: *What's your take on the Scriptures that encourage us to witness to others about our faith? Is that injunction for everybody or for those who are "called" to witness?*

MARY: Knowing the last thing Jesus said before He ascended into heaven was "Go into the entire world and preach the gospel," I'd say that was for all of us—everybody who follows Him as the Way, the Truth, and the Life. And can you imagine what it meant to the disciples who had followed Jesus? He was dead and buried, and it was over. Then suddenly, He was back. I think Jesus smiled and said softly, "Go tell your friends," and that's what they did. They went running out to tell everybody that He was alive. Then when those people heard it, they were excited, and the disciples smiled and said to them, "Go tell your friends." And so they did. And then two thousand years later we're still telling our friends because it's life-changing news.

You know, people say to me all the time at Women of Faith, "I love this. I had no idea." And I smile and say to them, "Go tell your friends."

LUCI: *Give me your best definition of a well-lived life. Do you have one?*

MARY: A well-lived life has to do with meaningful relationships with God and your loved ones. I think if you
lived in a shack by the side of the road or in the worst
neighborhood in the least-developed country in the
world or in a mansion but had meaningful relationships where you express love and know you are loved,
that's huge. By the same token, I believe people who
are consumed with themselves don't live very well.

And yes, I have a well-lived life. It's not perfectly
balanced, all my needs don't feel met, but I love many
wonderful people and I am loved. I have great work
that's making a huge difference in the world. I'm part
of a wonderful team. If nothing changed the rest of my
life, it would be fine with me. I have a great life. I could
do this the rest of my life—this team, this work, these
people, this dog.

›› EXAMPLE #4:
Peggy Wehmeyer

In every sense of the word, Peggy Wehmeyer blazed a pioneer
trail for every woman in America as the first religion reporter
for a major-market television station. After being the religion
reporter for WFAA-TV in Dallas for thirteen years, she went
to work for Peter Jennings on ABC's *World News Tonight*. It
was always a joy to watch this interesting, honest, dedicated
woman discuss faith and spiritual awareness and how they
interconnected with government and social policy. I rarely
missed one of Peter Jennings's broadcasts, and in large part it
was because of Peggy's contribution. Much of this Q and A
relates to that period in Peggy Wehmeyer's life.

As a forerunner in making religion relevant and alive, Peggy Wehmeyer talked with me candidly about what it takes to be on the cutting edge of that high-profile profession. Peggy has a compassionate heart and a servant spirit. With a background in journalism, theology, public relations, and world travel, she brings a storehouse of wisdom and a collection of compelling answers to many concerns.

LUCI: *Tell me briefly how you got the job with Peter Jennings.*

PEGGY: Peter realized religion had a lot to do with shaping the news, so he strongly felt the network needed a religion correspondent. But because management wasn't really interested, he kept taking the idea to the network—for about three years. He pushed so hard they finally agreed with it, under the condition that he find the reporter himself, which is not how it's normally done.

Peter personally looked for three months, but nobody was doing religion. Then he went to a Radio-Television News Directors Association convention in Miami, got up on stage, and said, "I need your help. Does anybody here know anyone in a major market who knows anything about religion?" Hundreds of news directors were there.

LUCI: *What are the major markets?*

PEGGY: Places like L.A., Philadelphia, Dallas, New York. I was the only one in the country covering religion, so people said to Peter, "Do you know about that woman in Dallas?" At that point in time, I had cut back to reporting a couple days a week to be home with my children. I was on the mommy track and barely on the career track, but he called me the next day. "This is Peter Jennings," he said, "and I have two questions for you: is it true that you cover religion, and are you open to a major life change?"

LUCI: *Did you believe it was really Peter Jennings?*

PEGGY: I did. I recognized his voice. It was amazing. Interestingly, I had never aspired to go to the networks. I was excited because I admired Peter so much. He was my journalism hero and my mentor. I answered, "Yes to number one, and two . . . I'm not sure."

He said, "Would you mind sending me a tape of your work?" That's what you do in our industry. The highlight of the whole episode was when he called again not long after I sent the tape, saying, "I loved your tape. How soon can you come to New York for some interviews?" It was one of the turning points in my career.

In my kind of career, the motto is *You're only as good as your last story*, and we really lived that. So when Peter called and said he liked my interview, I knew I had made it as a serious broadcast journalist.

LUCI: *Was taking the job an easy decision?*

PEGGY: I took the job after much soul-searching and prayer, because I had to decide if it was something God was calling me to do. It was so unusual and hard to imagine combining it with my family life.

Many of my colleagues were strategizing in every way they could to get to the network, and I was working part-time to be at home with my children, so when I got the job everybody was stunned. We were all standing around the newsroom one afternoon and somebody asked, "How come things like this always happen to you?" and another joked, since I was the religion reporter, "Must have been God." And I said, "Well, as a matter of fact, I think it was."

LUCI: *What do you think was the primary reason Peter chose you?*

PEGGY: I think he liked the tape because I was a solid journalist who was making religion real and relevant. It wasn't just about denominational politics or creeds; it was about living faith. It's a real challenge to take deep stories about religion and package them into a two-minute news segment that has to be subjected to the same tests of skepticism and verification as every other story in a broadcast.

LUCI: *What's the best preparation a woman can make to work in television news?*

PEGGY: If she's a Christian, two things come to mind: First, you have to be really good at your trade, the very best you can be at your skill so you reflect who God is in the excellence of your work. For me, it meant being a great, fair, balanced storyteller, a great writer, a good editor, and someone with the gift or knack of putting sound and word and pictures together. You have to hone that skill day in and day out, working and working at that.

I don't think you can stay grounded in that culture unless you know who *you* are as a person. My job was one of these glamorous jobs, and if that's what you want—to be a celebrity—forget it. It was never about glamour to me; it was about service—a sacred trust, serving the public, doing fair, honest, dependable journalism that people can count on.

Then secondly and equally as important, you have to be solidly grounded in your faith so you know who you are spiritually. If you don't, you get swept right up. It's a very powerful, intoxicating world. I had thought the temptations would be money and glamour, but the temptations come in vulnerable areas you would never expect. It's a wonderful career but a very worldly career. So if you don't know why you're there or who you are spiritually, you can lose yourself in it.

LUCI: *Did you ever feel your professional life disconnected from your spiritual life?*

PEGGY: Not really, because I believe that whether you're a mother, a TV anchorwoman, a secretary, if you believe you're called to serve God and reflect His glory, then it doesn't matter where you are or what you do. On the other hand, if you go into a profession in order to be somebody, which is common in businesses like mine, you're definitely going to feel a disconnect between your spiritual life and your professional life.

It's hard to pursue your own glory and God's glory at the same time.

Again, you need to be really grounded spiritually, and the way you do that is the same ol', same ol', regular spiritual discipline: time with God. And because of my personality, I needed accountability to a group of women I loved and with whom I shared everything. I had a speakerphone support group with three other powerful women. One served in the White House, one was a publisher, and another was in Christian ministry. We shared our struggles as mothers, wives, and career women and then prayed for each other.

Then I had another group of women friends in Dallas where I live, some of whom I've known since college, and they would just nail me when I was out of whack and I counted on that. I still meet with some of those women.

LUCI: *Which do you prefer, Peggy—developing a story so you can tell it succinctly or being in front of a camera on TV?*

PEGGY: Oh, that's easy. Being in front of the camera is nothing. It's just part of the trappings. That's how you get the story told. But going out, reporting, and putting the story together, letting the power of the story shape opinion and thought, well, that's where the sacred trust comes in. In network media, where millions of people get their news, you get to be the one to mold the story. The slightest nuance affects how people see the world.

LUCI: *Which is harder to manage: a high-profile career or a busy, involved family?*

PEGGY: I really juggled both, and that's a huge challenge. Personally I find the family part much easier because it is so instinctual. And I've been fortunate because I've never had any major trouble with my children. And I have a very involved, helpful husband. So even though we've certainly had our share of problems, I would say that managing a busy, active family is not as difficult for me as managing a high-profile career.

That's treacherous. It's like you're walking a tightrope and you could fall off because there are lots of unseen pits. Let me tell you something, Luci: it's hard to be a serious Christian in a high-profile, very secular profession because you're a fish out of water. First, you see the world differently than most of your colleagues; secondly, my job was to cover millions of Americans who also see the world through eyes of faith. That was a double whammy. People were suspect since I was a Christian covering religion. They assumed I had an agenda and couldn't be objective in my reporting. I always felt like I had to jump through three extra hoops to prove that I was, and that I didn't come from another planet, that the people I was covering really did exist and had brains and some of them actually did go to college.

It's hard when you need to be on a working team and you're viewed as an outsider. I couldn't be a part because I was so different. In your family, you belong.

LUCI: *How much do you trust your gut feeling about things? Do you think it's important to do that?*

PEGGY: Trusting your gut comes with maturing, with age. It's very important. You have to be careful, though, to distinguish between arrogance and what is really wisdom and truth coming through. I'm better at discerning that now, and when I go with my gut, I'm pleased. I also think it's good to know when *not* to trust your gut. A truly humble person is one who knows what he doesn't know. You have to be willing to say, "I'm sorry. I got that wrong."

LUCI: *How much importance do you put on the power of prayer in your work?*

PEGGY: Not very much. It's a weak area for me, because I'm a doer. Sometimes I mistake praying as passivity. My husband is a pray-er, and at times that bothers me. This morning, for instance, I'm leaving and wanting to say good-bye and he's on his knees. He prays about everything. And I just want to *do it*. I don't understand prayer. It's hard for me. When I pray, it's out of sheer obedience. I hate obeying when I don't understand something. I want to figure it all out. But I'm incredibly obedient.

LUCI: *I'm not sure prayer or obedience can be understood. Isn't prayer just something we're commanded to do?*

PEGGY: I'll tell you something . . . I went to a therapist once for something—this eighty-six-year-old woman—

gnarly, tough, rude, in your face. I went kind of for fun because everyone told me about her and I thought I'd just go sort some things out. She told me, "I have *never* met anybody who has so much passion, determination, and feeling going one direction and all this willpower to obey going in the other direction. There's such a clash going on inside of you (like in Romans 7). You are obedient to what you believe is true, no matter what you feel. It's unnatural." And I *loved* that!

I am so obedient. I was raised in a pretty sick, neurotic family—adulterous, divorced, alcoholic—so everything programmed in me genetically and environmentally is to go one way. Then I became a Christian and God said, "Whoa . . . you're going *this* way." I looked back and forth and said, "Well, it's one or the other. Okay, God, here I come." But all the time my genes and everything in me were pulling me to "come back over here."

I can look back on major milestones where I've obeyed when I wanted to do just the opposite, and I observe other people who did what I wanted to and think, *God was right*. I just keep obeying because I have enough altars along the way to know God's way is better than mine.

LUCI: *What do the words in the hymn "It Is Well with My Soul" mean to you?*

PEGGY: Those words mean I can be at peace with God even if my world is in chaos. No matter how much pain and suffering is in my marriage, or disappointments in my career, my soul is well. It may not mean I necessarily feel good, but it means everything's all right this side of heaven.

LUCI: *Does regret ever keep you from moving ahead or make you want to quit?*

PEGGY: Never. The reason I don't have regret is not because I'm such a great person, but because my temperament and personality style are forward-thinking: Win. Fight. Overcome. Regret and overcoming don't go together. Regret means depression to me, and my mother died of depression. She killed herself. I don't do the depression package.

One of my main missions in life is to be able to re-create in my children healthy, whole human beings. I want to break the chain of generations before me that didn't have the capacity to raise healthy children. It's very healing for me. Not only do I love being a mother, but it's very healing to see your legacy have a better shot at living well than you did.

LUCI: *Would you rather lead or follow?*

PEGGY: Lead.

LUCI: *Would you rather go out or stay home?*

PEGGY: Go out.

LUCI: *Would you rather work or play?*

PEGGY: Work.

LUCI: *Would you rather speak or listen?*

PEGGY: Speak. I'm embarrassed to say it and I regret that. (There's regret for you!) That's a real flaw of mine. I'm a good listener but I speak a lot. I'd rather be a listener—I wish I were a listener. My husband is a listener.

LUCI: *Would you rather give or take?*

PEGGY: I would say that it's a split. I used to be more of a taker, but I love to give.

LUCI: *Would you rather love or be loved?*

PEGGY: Do I have to be honest? Okay, it would depend on who you're talking about. Would it be with my children, my spouse, my friends? Um . . . that's a very embarrassing one to answer. I definitely love to love my children. And my husband? I probably enjoy being loved by him more than I enjoy loving him.

LUCI: *Are you ever driven to do more?*

PEGGY: Oh my gosh, *all the time.* This is one of my biggest problems. My greatest gift and my greatest weakness is longing for more. I'm rarely satisfied. But that's also been a gift in that I'm always pursuing excellence in a deeper relationship with God, a better marriage, better mothering. I want more of everything that's good and makes for a rich life.

LUCI: *Have you ever hit any roadblocks in your career?*

PEGGY: I've had personal roadblocks. The greatest are usually your own demons.

LUCI: *You mean like voices in your head telling you things?*

PEGGY: No, I mean your own vulnerability. I think your biggest obstacles are your own personal ones, not obstacles outside of yourself. This means, if God allows you to be successful and progress into places of influence and power, all your vulnerabilities will be revealed to you. How do you deal with your vulnerabilities when they are revealed? Do you run from them and deny them, which means you're going to get caught in a trap? Or do you face them, which is what repentance is, and allow God to make you whole?

Sometimes when you get to this place of success, you don't even know what your vulnerabilities are, so you're tested in these areas. The stakes are just a little higher when you're in a high-profile job with power and opportunity. The crash might be a little bigger if your vulnerabilities get you. I think we have to be willing to say no to some things that appear very fulfilling when God has called us to other things first. But it's not easy. I'm just a strong believer in doing what's right, whatever the cost.

LUCI: *Give me your definition of a well-lived life. Do you have one?*

PEGGY: Oh, I have a very well-lived life, for two reasons. The definition of the word *Israel* is "to struggle with God." I'm actually an Israelite—Jewish, by Jewish law, because my mother was a German Jew. I struggle ferociously to live well under God. So one reason my life is well lived is because I stay in the struggle. I don't run from pain or suffering. If you want to avoid pain, you cannot live well.

The second reason is because I rarely take no for an answer. Every time I walk into a situation and the door is closed, I knock. If they don't open it, sometimes I pound a little. Just because the door is closed doesn't mean God closed it. I've had incredible opportunities because I never gave up. I believe in asking for what you want and what you believe God is calling you to.

›› EXAMPLE #5:
CeCe Winans

A family with ten children, the Winans family may not have had their own ball team, but they certainly had their own opera, with drama, beauty, music, and lyrics all designed and written by God Himself. Can't you just picture the joy and challenges of that busy household? We've all read rave reviews and heard about the many awards that CeCe Winans has earned, but being able to talk with her one-on-one, face-to-face was the thrill of a lifetime. We showed up together at Starbucks in our blue jeans and chatted like two friends swapping stories over the back fence. Every moment was fun. I'll never forget it.

CeCe has one of the most mesmerizing voices that ever wafted across the airwaves, yet it's not just her singing that makes her the admired woman she is. It's her levelheadedness, her delight in being a mother, her humor, her sympathy for people, and her integration with life. It's her ability to lift us out of our busy, everyday circumstances into a calm, holy place. She's what the Italians refer to as *simpatico*—a person with the innate ability to keep both feet on the ground while walking on air. What a contagious spirit! With a light that shines from the inside, she leads the way in the direction we all want to go and invites us to come with her.

LUCI: *I know you come from a singing family, CeCe. Did you sing harmony growing up, like from one bedroom to another—just yell out and start singing?*

CECE: Yes. That's exactly what we did, as far back as I can remember. My parents both sing. That's how they met: singing in a chorus. I have nine siblings: seven boys straight, and I'm the first girl. And everybody sings!

My father trained us to sing harmony when we were kids. Actually, when my brothers were little they couldn't go to bed unless they got the notes right. So growing up, we were always singing at home, in the choir too. My mother and father both played the piano.

LUCI: *Was it always sacred music?*

CeCe: Always sacred—that's the only music our parents allowed us to have in the house.

Luci: *Does your husband sing? And your children?*

CeCe: Um . . . Alvin cannot sing at all. I repeat: *at all.*

Luci: *Does he try?*

CeCe: Well, he loves the Lord, so sometimes he'll bust out in a song. It's not in tune, but I'm sure the Lord loves to hear it. Both of my kids sing. My son is majoring in music in college. He loves to sing, dance, write—you name it. He's always loved it, and he's very good.

Luci: *I understand you now have a recording company. Tell me a little bit about that.*

CeCe: The name of it is Pure Springs Gospel, and I've had it now for about four or five years. We have two other artists on the label besides me: my home-church choir, the Born Again Church Choir; and a wonderful artist named Vicky Yohe. We have a small staff and a lot of different deals with other major labels for distribution, but we're doing very well.

Luci: *You probably have a lot of competition here in Nashville.*

CeCe: Yes, but that's okay. We welcome it.

Luci: *You've been described as a worship leader, CeCe. Tell me what that means to you.*

CeCe: I would describe myself as just one who loves to worship. I think the leading comes when you're doing what you love to do and what you're called to do. And hopefully I'm teaching others to do it—encouraging others to do it.

Luci: *Is that your goal, your desire—to encourage the audi-ence to join you in worship?*

CeCe: That's definitely my goal every time I take the stage. It's to take people where I feel like I need to take them.

Luci: *Do you enjoy it and all that goes with it?*

CeCe: I love it—once I'm into it. I'm not crazy about every-thing that goes with it, traveling and so on, but I love doing it.

Luci: *Well, we love you, CeCe, and we'll come wherever you are. We also love your backup group. I think they're fabulous. You guys are Gladys Knight and the Pips. I always tell them that. Do you know Gladys Knight?*

CeCe: Yes, I do.

Luci: *Do you know "Midnight Train to Georgia"?*

CeCe: Oh, are you kidding?

LUCI: *I want that song sung at my funeral or my wedding, whichever comes first. So if you could work that out, it'd be great. Where'd you find your backup group?*

CECE: They're awesome, and they all belong to my church.

LUCI: *Choir members.*

CECE: Actually, no. They never sang in the choir. You know, I've always had background singers ever since I've been singing, and this group has been with me three or four years. But out of twenty years, that's not a long time. I've always liked having people in the back that sang much better than I do. They're very sweet and very funny. They keep me laughing.

LUCI: *Jerard's the only guy. Is he tenor or bass? I can't tell. And that range! I think he makes up notes!*

CECE: Oh yes, on the spot. And he loves being "the guy" at Women of Faith. He milks it a lot. Actually, we just sang in California. Andraé Crouch came to our concert and we had a great time. But he was telling Jerard and the background singers how much he loved him. That was in the first half. So in the second half I think they did a lot of extra things because Andraé was in the house. I was like, "Wait a minute."

LUCI: *Before you go out onstage to sing, what do you do to prepare spiritually?*

CeCe: Just really focus. We always have prayer and devotions. One of the background singers often leads our devotions on the road. She's awesome in the Word of God, very nurturing and sweet. But I really just try to come out of myself. I know that might sound weird, but I never would have chosen this for myself. I'm more comfortable in the background. If I could stay home and be in the choir or do praise and worship in the church, that would be fabulous for me.

Luci: You'd be content to be at home? You don't need to be a star.

CeCe: Oh no. This is so totally not me.

Luci: So when you prepare, you try to just forget yourself?

CeCe: Yes, because I realize when people come, they're not there to see me. They're there to see what I have in me. I have to realize that what is in me is so much greater than me. So that's what we try to do: just focus on the presence of the Lord and what He wants to happen. That's why the backup group is really great. They're not just talented; they have the same heart and the same goals that I do. Therefore, we're a team.

Luci: As an attentive mother, do you ever wish you didn't have this public ministry?

CeCe: Oh yeah, definitely. I've always wished that. The Lord has always worked it out where I wasn't away from my kids that long. Of course, every moment is precious with your children. So if you feel like you miss one moment, you think, *Oh, this is awful.* But I always had my mom and my mother-in-law when the children were small, and when we went on tours, I put them on the tour bus with me. Then I put them in homeschool for a few years before they went into that teenage thing, where they all lose their minds. So I was like, "Uh-huh, y'all are comin' with me." The Lord provided a wonderful young lady—my assistant—who started out being their homeschool teacher. So that's what we did—we traveled on the bus and had a great time. And when they got a little older, they wanted to go back to school. Actually, we kicked them out of homeschool.

LUCI: *What do your kids think of your being famous?*

CeCe: It's funny. They are very different from each other. My son has wanted to be onstage ever since he was little. He's wanted to wear black because background singers wear black. And my daughter was always asking, "Is this your last song? Can we please go home?" She can sing, but she's not interested in singing. She likes sports and shopping. She's sixteen. She likes music but is much more interested in dancing. But we'll see in a few years.

LUCI: *What keeps you going when you'd rather not?*

CeCe: God's people. All the responses that I get—the letters, phone calls, e-mails. They say, "I was contemplating suicide, but I heard one of your songs and decided to give life another try." That's what keeps me doing what I do—when you know you're doing more than entertaining people, that you really make a difference. It's encouraging to know people begin to understand and see the value in serving the Lord and worshiping the Lord. Having the Lord in your life makes all the difference, so if I can spread that to somebody, then a life is being touched. Somebody is changing.

LUCI: *What's the most important thing needed in worship?*

CECE: A heart. If you have a heart that's passionate about our Creator, that's worship. It's a lifestyle. That's why when my husband's singing around the house, I think, "Lord, this is beautiful to You."

LUCI: *I think there's something so unique and rhythmical in black singers, and we don't have it. I'd like to not be a white girl so I can sing like you're singing. It's almost enviable, because it's so heartfelt with the blacks. It comes from inside you. You don't get off pitch or rhythm; you make up stuff along the way. Is there anything we whites can do to get it? Where does it come from, CeCe? Is it heritage or culture?*

CECE: I think it does have a lot to do with where we come from—our heritage. I also think it's God-given. Honestly, I see it in a lot of different cultures; maybe not as much as in ours, but it's there. I think for a long time, because of the different barriers, people said black people could sing and dance, and white people couldn't. But I've seen it all over the world. You also have to know, Luci, that a lot of people in our culture don't sing and don't dance. So to me, it's not really a color thing. It's a gift.

LUCI: *Can people do it if they really want to?*

CECE: No. Some people really want to and can't. For example, when we were growing up, we couldn't afford any type of lessons. We couldn't afford to go and learn how to read music. There were a lot of things we didn't have, so we just made things up. We had to create and go with what we felt. Other people would read the notes, but that was it. They went to school for that. Even though schooling's a great thing, it's limiting sometimes because that's what you learn and that's all.

LUCI: *I just saw the big program Oprah did about AIDS in South Africa. On that show she was singing and dancing, and I thought, Where does she get that rhythm? It's in her heart and soul.*

CECE: Oprah's funny. She loves music, and she's a joy to watch. That's one of the things I try to get across to people. They'll say, "I've never been able to really cut loose, to be free in worship and free in praise." I think it's important that you get to a place where you're free and can let yourself go. This is what you see in Oprah. When we stop worrying about doing everything just right, the expression of freedom will come from inside, and that's so much more powerful than if you do everything right. This is why I know expression is not a color thing—it's a freedom thing.

LUCI: *If you could give advice to a young singer just starting out in a public career, what would you say to her?*

CECE: The first thing I would encourage her to do is to really have a lifestyle behind the song. You have to be grounded and rooted. When you're grounded, no matter what comes, you're going to stand. The most important thing is the relationship with the Lord.

Number two would be to just be who you are. Nobody can beat you at who you are. A lot of times people will come into the industry because of other people who have inspired them, which is okay. But don't try to be them, because the Lord creates us differently for a reason. We're all uniquely made, and we need to be ourselves. It's going to be much easier being who we are as opposed to being somebody we're not.

Number three, have fun. Enjoy it. Enjoy the ride.

And finally, learn to appreciate every door that opens and every door that closes. A lot of time we spend frustrated, thinking we should have done this or done that, but the Lord really does order our footsteps. That's a real relief to me. It's a peace nobody can take away when you know the Lord orders your steps. So I've learned to praise Him in all situations because I know for a fact that He's going to take care of me.

LUCI: *Was it hard to get to the place of knowing all that?*

CeCe: Yes, it was very hard. But it's a faith walk. And it's so much more fun when you get to this place. It's stress-free.

Luci: *What's your favorite Scripture and why?*

CeCe: I have a lot of favorites, but I would have to say Philippians 4:13: "I can do all things through Christ who strengthens me." I always have to be reminded I cannot do things in my own strength. When I realize there's no weakness in Him, I grab hold and say, "I can do this." I can be a mother of teenagers; I can be on the road; I can make it.

The longer I walk with the Lord, the more I realize His Word is true, that He is right all the time . . . and that everything will be okay even though it may seem very dark. It's a wonderful Scripture!

Luci: *Which requires more patience or wisdom from you: people who are rude or people who are late?*

CeCe: Probably rude. Rude is rough. But I know love conquers all, so I kind of get joy out of throwing love on top of rude people, and they don't know what to do with that. You know, it's hard to continue to be rude when someone is being nice back.

Luci: *Which requires more patience or wisdom from you: people who don't keep their word or people who won't commit?*

CeCe: People who don't keep their word, because integrity is very important.

LUCI: *Which is harder to balance: being a good mother or being a disciplined Christian?*

CECE: A disciplined Christian. I wouldn't say it's easy to be a good mother, but it's easier. I don't think a lot of people are disciplined the way they should be in following the Father. I just know for a fact that being a disciplined Christian helps you be everything you need to be. In being a mom, for example, you need wisdom in raising your children, and where else are you going to get that but from the Father? There have been times the Holy Spirit revealed to me certain things I could say to my kids: "Don't even try it, because the Holy Spirit will tell me everything I need to know about y'all. I know exactly what you're doing and what you're thinking—everything." So it's been proven to be true. That's definitely the key.

LUCI: *What are the ingredients most needed to maintain a balanced, passionate, fulfilled life?*

CECE: Well, you have to go to the Lord first. I don't know how people accomplish anything without putting Him first. He gives you wisdom in every area of your life.

Laughter is very important. If you can't laugh, then you're miserable. Patience is a must-have ingredient. Just wait and, in time, things will happen. And I think it helps to be positive, to always look at things as half-full instead of half-empty. When you expect a blessing, you receive a blessing.

LUCI: *Give me your best definition of a well-lived life. Do you have one? Does anybody have one?*

CECE: I think some people have them. That's a hard question. I think I have one, but it could be much better. A well-lived life is when you can live in the moment, absorb today, get hold of today and appreciate it. I don't think I do that enough because I'm always planning. I'm always thinking about what I have to do next. You know, if you're worried about next week, you don't appreciate this week. I think a well-lived life is really living fully every moment and enjoying it.

I'm trying to think if I know anybody like that. Let's see . . . my husband is probably better than I am. He takes it easy; he doesn't get anxious about what's going to happen. That's good for me, and I need to be more like that.

LUCI: *Does Alvin ever say, "Let's just enjoy this"?*

CECE: Yes. Maybe men are more like that than women. We're always trying to get this or that together. But if you can just absorb each moment, you're enjoying a well-lived life.

6 the niche

FINALLY, FULFILLMENT!

*It is not what I do that matters, but what a
sovereign God chooses to do through me.
God doesn't want worldly successes. He
wants me. He wants my heart in submission
to Him. Life is not just a few years to spend
on self-indulgence and career advancement.
It's a privilege, a responsibility, a steward-
ship to be lived according to a much higher
calling—God's calling. This alone gives true
meaning to life.*

—Elizabeth Dole
National Prayer Breakfast Address, 1987

Magda Olivero lives in Milan, Italy, and she invited my
friend Charlotte and me to lunch in her apartment. An eleva-
tor took us to the second floor, where the door opened and we
stepped into another world: antiques, paintings, Persian rugs,
rare books, gorgeous furnishings, and an enormous grand
piano that dominated the living room. On every wall and in
every hand-carved cabinet was memorabilia from this great
singer's years with the opera, including gifts from various

nations. She gave us a tour as we awaited the arrival of her husband, Aldo, who was joining us for lunch.

Everything spoke of quality: the china, the crystal, the furnishings, the maid, the music. Even the conversation was nourishment for the mind and heart. But that was only the beginning.

After a delicious meal Aldo went back to work, and Magda's personal chauffeur drove us to Lake Como for the afternoon. This breathtaking area of northern Italy is about twenty-five miles from Milan. Magda especially wanted us to see the famous Villa d'Este, built in 1550, that was situated beside the lake. She was our guide as we walked around.

There were four of us: Magda, the driver, my friend Charlotte, and myself. We talked about lots of things in both English and Italian, trying to make ourselves understood with sign language. (As you can imagine, it helps immeasurably in Italian/English conversations to use your hands.)

Admittedly, I occasionally went off on my own musings: *Pinch yourself, Luci. Are you really here? With Magda Olivero, the Magda Olivero? Savor this moment, kid. You're on top of the world.*

When we arrived at the lake, I was indeed sittin' on top of the world. Lake Como lies at an altitude of 650 feet, in a depression surrounded by mountains reaching from two thousand to eight thousand feet, snowcapped and stunningly beautiful. The day was clear, with a chill in the April air. The first blush of spring was on branches of oleander, chestnut, fig, and pomegranate trees that lined the lake.

Hotel officials greeted Magda warmly when we walked in. They knew her well and escorted us to a table near the window overlooking the lake, while our driver waited in the car.

We ordered tea. My mind left the scene again: *This is unbelievable. How can this famous woman, with all she has to do, take time to leisurely show us Lake Como? Give up an afternoon? Treat us like royalty? What kind of woman is this?*

Magda told us the lake was famous for its natural beauty. Sportsmen flocked there annually to fish. A private club for boating and swimming was available. Standing on the shore, one can look to the north and see the Swiss Alps.

Our friend loved this place. She liked to recall fond memories of earlier visits. And the people at the hotel obviously loved her; they treated her like the great lady she is.

It's no wonder. Magda Olivero had enjoyed a remarkable opera career in Europe. Her sensitive interpretations of various roles had made her famous worldwide. At the time, Charlotte and I had known her only a year; we had been working with the Dallas Opera Company when Magda made her American debut there in 1967. But that day we felt like two of the most important people in her life. We didn't realize until later, as we had opportunity to know her better, that Magda made everybody feel this way.

We had heard how famous composers had either written specific works or resurrected earlier compositions just for her vocal and dramatic gifts. In turn, she told them she'd do the part as the *umile ancella* (humble servant) of the composer.

And there we were, the two of us—guests of this famous lady in this gorgeous spot. That day, that place, those feelings are etched in my memory forever.

Two years later while vacationing in Europe, I visited Magda again at her summer home in Rapallo. It's a small, picturesque village near Portofino in that upper portion of the Italian boot that spills over in small treasure towns, like toys out of a Christmas stocking. Every winding road has an unexpected surprise of foliage and color, and we simply got drunk with all the beauty.

One afternoon I was sitting at a picture window overlooking this visual delight. Overcome by it all—the view, the beauty, the fact that I was Magda's friend—I heard myself ask, "Magda, how does it feel to be you?"

She looked at me quizzically. I'm sure she was caught off guard by such a forthright question. "What do you mean?"

"How can I say it . . ." I thought for a minute, looking out the window, trying to gather up every Italian word I'd ever learned. Using sign language to enhance my efforts, I continued, "Look at you. You have everything: two beautiful homes, lovely furnishings, an enviable career, fame, money, a husband who adores you, audiences who laud you and fall at your feet, power—everything. I mean, it's fantastic. How does it feel to be such a successful woman?"

She had a very sweet expression on her face and in her eyes as I ticked off the things I both admired and envied. When I finally stopped rambling and let her get a word in, she responded to my questions with the most gracious answer.

Slowly, she began with the wave of her hand, "Luci, this isn't success—all these things. It's nice to have them, don't misunderstand me. I love things, and it's gratifying to know I can live comfortably, surrounded by beauty.

"It's nice not to have material needs, but I don't call this success. To me, success is giving myself to the public. It's knowing I've touched people with talent—my singing and acting, my life. It's the effect I have on the people who come to hear me sing, the people I've made richer because they heard me. That's success.

"When I was young, I used to think success was having all these things, but it's not. Once I found that out, I was a new person. I then had something really important.

"You know, Luci, when I die I'd like to die onstage giving myself, my all, to my public. That's the greatest fulfillment there is, to think that what I have inside can make a difference to somebody else. That's what life is all about."

I just sat there. This was a revelation that changed my thinking forever, given from a "great depth of being," as Emerson says. I was in my thirties then, and now, looking back four decades later, I realize how young I was. I knew inside, though, that Magda was right.

I simply *loved* that answer, and from that moment on I began to view success and professionalism differently. I have never looked back. Something clicked in my head that day. My brain took a picture of that answer and developed it into my life.

There's a world of people out there operating under the illusion that they've finally reached their professional niche because they have a title and a great deal of money, wield a lot of power, are surrounded by a hefty number of expensive trappings, control a lot of people, burn the midnight oil at the office, and intimidate others with their presence. They've built for themselves a bright and shining empire. But what about those of us outside their castle? What about people they've been in contact with every day?

Contrary to public opinion, life doesn't begin and end in ourselves. Sometimes we think people don't notice when we shortchange them by our rudeness, or they're not aware of our lack of integrity when we cheat them out of our very best.

Read the words of newscaster Linda Ellerbee, who deals

with these issues every day in the world of television: "It's up to those of us who work in the business to be honest reporters—and to learn our craft to make sure that we know how to write, that we produce television and not radio, and that we leave a little something for our audience to do."[1]

Ms. Ellerbee is not suggesting that the people to whom we give ourselves have no responsibility to make wise use of the information we pass on to them. On the contrary, she's trying to show that when we give our best, others will know it and will respond with their best. Integrity breeds integrity.

She goes on: "We at our end have to put in the best we have to offer, because at the other end is a viewer who deserves the best—and knows the difference. That viewer is our audience, even if it's an audience of one, which it's not."[2]

It's our obligation as Christian professionals to give our best to others, adding dimensions to their lives so they'll want to give their best to those they meet. And don't kid yourself; your public—those you encounter every day—knows when it's getting the best from you. They can tell fresh from leftover.

Occasionally I'm asked, "How does it feel to be in your professional niche, Luci?" The inquirer isn't asking, "What are the steps in getting there?" or "How long does it take to arrive?" Those are very different questions. When someone asks how it *feels*, she's asking for an emotional response, not an objective one. It's like my asking Magda, "How does it *feel* to be you?"

I don't think that's an easy question to answer because reducing emotions to words is inadequate. Words are tools of the mind, not the heart. But I've thought about that question for years and have finally come up with an answer, although I'm forced to use words to describe it.

I trust this down-to-earth example will capture what I feel. It's as if I'm a hot apple muffin.

I'll explain.

One of my favorite foods on earth is fresh, hot, homemade apple muffins. I make them occasionally when I have time and enjoy them with a fresh-brewed pot of Starbucks. I take the muffin, the coffee, and the newspaper, and sit on my patio (sometimes with the neighborhood cats), relishing the beginning of a new day. All my senses are pleased. Complete satisfaction.

When you bake apple muffins, you put all the ingredients together: flour, butter, baking powder, eggs, milk, apples, a pinch of cinnamon, vanilla, and so on. All these go into a bowl to be blended together. But this blending doesn't make the muffins; it only makes the mixture, the goop. So you spoon the goop into muffin tins and then put the tins in the oven.

A strange metamorphosis takes place. The heat from the oven changes the mixture into edible food. When they're done, the finished muffins don't look like the original ingredients in the mixing bowl. In the bowl, they're just dead weight. But the mixture undergoes a change by the addition of heat, and when the time is right, voilà: irresistible apple muffins. When that muffin is eaten, it's happy because it's doing that for which it was made, and the eater is happy because her hunger is assuaged.

My professional life is a mixture. It has a great deal of hard work in it, taking hours of time, concentration, discipline, and sacrifice. To be a working woman involves risktaking and numerous transitions. It demands that I use my head and my heart. It requires different ingredients: delegation, relegation, deferment, courage, humor, a pinch of craziness, a spoonful of sugar. All those things and more.

But all this without heat is nothing more than just so much lifeless goop—dead weight. Who wants it?

The hungry person who comes in contact with my mixture of traits won't be satisfied with lifelessness. She wants my blend, hot out of the oven. Only the heat of life and testing and experience can give the one in need the taste that satisfies. The energy of the Holy Spirit comes through my enduring the heat. It's the most important element to being irresistible.

We can give ourselves to the people around us in a meaningful, eternal, fulfilling way when we permit ourselves to be transformed by God's energy. We've got to stay hot, tasty, and fresh if we're to be food for the hungry.

Before Oprah Winfrey became the icon she is today, I went with a group of friends to see her at a local university. You talk about a hot apple muffin—wow! Full of energy, humor, and warmth, she was thoroughly captivating to a sold-out house. For an hour, she told us about her life, her thoughts, and some of the difficulties she's come through in her rise to being a talk-show host. She did several dramatic readings and brought the house down.

Everybody in our group was deeply moved and entertained. Oprah discussed her faith, her trust in God, her dependence upon the Scriptures, her professional aspirations. Nobody in the audience wanted the evening to end.

About thirty minutes before the close of her program, Oprah took questions from the floor. Hands shot up everywhere. Men, women, blacks, whites, young people, older people—everybody had questions.

One was, "Oprah, to what do you attribute your success?" She said, "I think it's the fact that I try to treat people the way I want to be treated. That's what makes anybody successful.

Every one of you out there can be great if you treat people with love and respect and understanding. You may not be *famous*, but you can be great." As she was talking, I thought about Luke 9:48, which clearly teaches that our care for others is the measure of greatness.

Oprah went on to say that if you have confidence in yourself, mixed with faith in God, there's no limit to what you can do. I cheered. My sentiments exactly! Oprah gave herself to her public, and we ate her up.

For those of us who are Christian working women, there are some wonderful verses in Matthew 20 that should be our guide for leadership. Jesus said:

> Among the heathen, kings are tyrants and each minor official lords it over those beneath him. But among you it is quite different. Anyone wanting to be a leader among you must be your servant. And if you want to be right at the top, you must serve like a slave. Your attitude must be like my own, for I, the Messiah, did not come to be served, but to serve, and to give my life as a ransom for many. (Matthew 20:25–28, TLB)

Boy! Just compare that with the information that's often touted on how to rise to the top of your professional ladder. It's not only different; it's antithetical! No two concepts could be more opposite. Jesus calls us to committed servanthood, while the world calls us to constant striving.

We often balk at servanthood. The idea of serving like a slave conjures up in our mind a very distasteful image. Rare is the person who wants to know, "What can I *give*?" Most of us want to know, "What can I *get*?"

But let me remind us again—each one of us, myself included—that the backbone of true professionalism is character, not empire. Therein lies the key to embracing servanthood gladly.

True professionalism, as you have seen from this book and can perhaps testify from your own life, is contrary to the steps that the world orders. It's not by might or power, but by tranquillity mixed with grace. It's not by intimidation, but by courage mixed with vulnerability. It's not by workaholism, but by constancy mixed with balance. And it's not by a system of hierarchy, but by democracy mixed with servanthood. In every case it is contrary to the world. But it works.

A magazine article appeared several years ago that told of a twenty-nine-year-old man named Paul, who was dying of AIDS, and of how his office force rallied around him from the moment they suspected the nature of his illness until the day he died. "Where 'Boss' Stops and 'Friend' Begins" was a loving account of triumph in the midst of tragedy.

As a copyeditor for a national magazine, Paul was vague about symptoms that forced him to have a series of medical tests. He referred to the doctor's diagnosis as "stomach problems." However, as his condition worsened, his coworkers became like family to him. Recognizing fear in his eyes and his unusual behavior, Paul's fellow employees, instead of backing off, demonstrated constant concern and care. When he was afraid of being fired because of missing so much work, they reassured him of his position as a valued member of the team. When Mike, the managing editor, had to assume some of Paul's duties, he was careful not to hurt Paul's feelings. Mike told Paul he "had a few extra minutes to kill and would welcome the work." Paul's supervisor took him to lunch at his favorite restaurant, knowing the bright Christmas decorations would lift his spirits. She also wanted to give him a pep talk, to tell him he was doing excellent work in spite of his difficult circumstances.

Later, Paul told his friends he had cancer of the stomach. When his chemotherapy treatments left him nauseated and dizzy, he had a hard time getting to work by nine o'clock. Office staff told him not to worry about it. Paul found little gifts awaiting his arrival: flowers, notes, homemade meals. One person offered to help him with his weekly grocery shopping. Another, trying to boost Paul's morale, brought bagels and orange juice to the office on beautiful days, saying she thought everyone should celebrate.

Paul's illness progressed, and he was admitted to a hospital for treatment. The office staff visited him regularly, focusing their attention solely on Paul, trying to be sensitive to his feelings and his need to know everything that happened in the office during his absence. Because he felt guilty about missing so much work, the staff bagged up poetry that readers had submitted and took the bags to Paul, telling him they desperately needed him to read the poems and comment on them. And Paul was delighted to have something to do—to feel needed.

During this period, Paul's office friends became a sounding board for his anger concerning his disease—anger directed at anyone who happened to visit. As Paul deteriorated physically, his friends experienced emotional deterioration. Everyone was on edge. Tempers flared. Each person was trying to deal with bottled-up emotions for a dying coworker. But they continued to stand by him.

Ultimately Paul had to be replaced. With only two years of service, Paul was offered a fully paid leave of absence. After months of hospital stays, he finally admitted to his boss the truth about his illness. He had known for over a year that he had AIDS. The editor confessed that from the beginning, she had known this down deep in her heart.

The love and caring at that point intensified. Fellow employees visited Paul as often as they could. When they weren't able to go because of colds or flu, they made elaborate cards or sent baskets of goodies to Paul's hospital room.

There were days that Paul's anger and fear overwhelmed him, making him cutting and bitter. When friends called, he hung up on them. But *never* did Paul's former coworkers reject him or stop visiting. They constantly assured him that they loved him, cared for him, remembered him. In every possible way they tried to get across, "We'll be there for you."

His friends read poetry to him, prayed for him, even agreed to assume responsibility for his body after death, when his parents could not be reached. During the last few hours of his life, his fellow workers kept a candlelight vigil at his bedside. In the early hours of one New Year's Eve Day, Paul died, the victim of a horrible disease but the recipient of unconditional love and affection.[3]

That's character and professionalism to the max, lived out in the workplace. It's possible for any of us to achieve that kind of lifestyle at the office once we realize our proper response to people's needs. As Christian women in the professional world, it is our duty—dare I say our mission in life?—to be there for people. It is our highest calling. It's the most important part of our professional niche.

It's the hope for this world.

When Corazon Aquino, the fifty-three-year-old leader of fifty-five million people, was elected president in the Republic of the Philippines, she brought a new hope and a new courage to that nation. "I am not embarrassed to tell you that I believe in miracles," she declared frankly.

> God has a plan for all of us, and it is for each of us to find out what that plan is. I can tell you that I never thought the plan was for me to be president. But it seems it is—it has been necessary to have a woman in this position. Women are less liable to resort to violence than men, and at this time in my country's history, what is really needed is a man or woman of peace.[4]

The Christian professional woman is a woman of peace. She is a woman who believes in miracles. From her first days of wandering and wondering to the arrival at her desired destination, she is one who pursues excellence. She may fall, she may be sidetracked, she may even be blocked in for a time, but she never gives up. With heart, courage, brains, and faith, she continually progresses, recognizing her abilities and strengths come from God. And when her deepest joy becomes giving her life away to others, she will have truly found her place of greatest contribution.

notes

chapter 1

1. Paul Ciotti, "A Walk in the Woods," *Los Angeles Times Magazine*, December 22, 1985, 23, 24, 36, 38.
2. Jane Arnold, "The Columnists," *Savvy*, October 1985, 36–40.
3. Jacqueline Giambanco, "Designing a Corporate Image," *Working Woman*, July 1985, 80–82.

chapter 2

1. Beverly Sills, *Bubbles* (New York: Bobbs-Merrill Co., 1976), 209.
2. Ibid., 114.
3. Ibid., 224.
4. Kaylan Pickford, *Always a Woman* (New York: Bantam Books, 1982).
5. Ibid.
6. Ibid.
7. E. F. Wells, *Successful Supervisor* (Chicago: Dartnell Corp., 1985).
8. William Arthur Ward, "I Will Do More," *Successful Supervisor* (Chicago: Dartnell Corp., 1986). Used by permission of the author.
9. Samuel Chotzinoff, *A Little Night Music* (New York: Harper & Row, 1964), 89–90.

10. Sophia Loren, *Women and Beauty* (New York: William Morrow *and* Co., 1984), 189–91.

11. "The Beautiful Dream," *Successful Supervisor* (1986).

chapter 3

1. Charles R. Swindoll, *Three Steps Forward, Two Steps Back* (Nashville: Thomas Nelson Publishers, 1980), 17–18.

2. Mary C. Crowley in *America's New Women Entrepreneurs*, ed. Patricia Harrison (Washington, D.C.: Acropolis Books, 1986), 79.

3. Linda Swindall, "Delegate, Delegate!" *Working Woman*, July 1985, 23.

4. Douglas LaBier, *Modern Madness: The Emotional Fallout of Success* (Reading, Mass.: Addison-Wesley Publishing Co., 1986), 76.

5. Ibid., 77.

6. Heather Evans, "The Plight of the 'Corporate Nun,'" *Working Woman*, November 1984, 63.

7. Gail Sheehy, *Passages* (New York: Bantam Books, 1984), 513.

8. Joan Kufrin, *Uncommon Women* (Piscataway, N.J.: New Century Publishers, 1981), 30.

chapter 4

1. Pauline Clance, quoted in Elizabeth Christian, "'Fakes' Scared of Being Found Out," *Los Angeles Times*, December 8, 1985.

2. Dale Hanson Bourke, "Danuta Soderman: Can We Talk?" *Today's Christian Woman*, January/February 1987, 34.

3. Ibid.

4. Daniel Taylor, *The Myth of Certainty* (Waco, Texas: Word Books, 1986), 113.

5. Ibid., 123–24.

6. Gail Sheehy, *Pathfinders* (New York: William Morrow, 1981), 445.

7. Donna Kordela, "Small Talk: Chitchat That Leads to Serious Discussion," *The Executive Female*, December 1985, 33.

8. Marilyn Meberg, *Choosing the Amusing* (Portland: Multnomah Press, 1986), 58.

9. Ibid., 59.

10. Ibid., 71–73.

11. Marilyn Loden, "Managing the Woman's Way," *Newsweek*, March 17, 1986, 46.

chapter 6

1. Linda Ellerbee, *And So It Goes: Adventures in Television* (New York: G. P. Putnam's Sons, 1986), 250.

2. Ibid.

3. Leah Booth, "Where 'Boss' Stops and 'Friend' Begins," *Working Woman*, February 1987, 70–74, 110.

4. Pico Iyer, "Cory—Woman of the Year," *Time*, January 5, 1987, 18–33.

about the author

Committed to a life of joy, adventure, and celebration, speaker and author LUCI SWINDOLL has long been provoking smiles and inciting laughter in audiences around the world. One of the pioneering women authors in the contemporary Christian book market, Luci wrote, among other classic titles, *You Bring the Confetti, God Brings the Joy* and *I Married Adventure*. Earlier in her career, Luci served as an executive at Mobil Oil Corporation, then as Vice President of Public Relations at Insight for Living, the international radio ministry of her brother, Chuck Swindoll. Today, she continues to touch lives through her vigorous speaking schedule with Women of Faith®.

EXTRAORDINARY*faith*

CONFERENCE *2005*

2005 EVENT CITIES & SPECIAL GUESTS

NATIONAL
CONFERENCE
LAS VEGAS, NV
FEBRUARY 17-19
Thomas & Mack Center

NATIONAL
CONFERENCE
FT. LAUDERDALE, FL
FEBRUARY 24-26
Office Depot Center

SHREVEPORT, LA
APRIL 1-2
CenturyTel Center
Sandi Patty,
Chonda Pierce,
Jennifer Rothschild

HOUSTON, TX
APRIL 8-9
Toyota Center
Kristin Chenoweth,
Natalie Grant,
Jennifer Rothschild

COLUMBUS, OH
APRIL 15-16
Nationwide Arena
Avalon,
Kristin Chenoweth,
Nichole Nordeman

BILLINGS, MT
MAY 13-14
MetraPark
Sandi Patty,
Chonda Pierce,
Jennifer Rothschild

PITTSBURGH, PA
MAY 20-21
Mellon Arena
Natalie Grant,
Nichole Nordeman,
Chonda Pierce

KANSAS CITY, MO
JUNE 3-4
Kemper Arena
Natalie Grant,
Chonda Pierce,
Jennifer Rothschild

ST. LOUIS, MO
JUNE 17-18
Savvis Center
Avalon,
Nichole Nordeman,
Chonda Pierce

CANADA &
NEW ENGLAND
CRUISE
JUNE 25 – JULY 2
Tammy Trent

ATLANTA, GA
JULY 8-9
Philips Arena
Natalie Grant,
Sherri Shepherd,
Tammy Trent

FT. WAYNE, IN
JULY 15-16
Allen County War
Memorial Coliseum
Sandi Patty,
Chonda Pierce,
Jennifer Rothschild

DETROIT, MI
JULY 22-23
Palace of Auburn Hills
Sherri Shepherd,
Tammy Trent,
CeCe Winans

WASHINGTON, DC
JULY 29-30
MCI Center
Natalie Grant,
Nichole Nordeman,
Sherri Shepherd

SACRAMENTO, CA
AUGUST 5-6
ARCO Arena
Avalon,
Kristin Chenoweth,
Tammy Trent

PORTLAND, OR
AUGUST 12-13
Rose Garden Arena
Kristin Chenoweth,
Natalie Grant,
Tammy Trent

DENVER, CO
AUGUST 19-20
Pepsi Center
Avalon,
Kristin Chenoweth,
Nichole Nordeman

DALLAS, TX
AUGUST 26-27
American Airlines Center
Avalon,
Kristin Chenoweth,
Nichole Nordeman

ANAHEIM, CA
SEPTEMBER 9-10
Arrowhead Pond
Avalon, Chonda Pierce,
Tammy Trent

PHILADELPHIA, PA
SEPTEMBER 16-17
Wachovia Center
Kathie Lee Gifford,
Natalie Grant,
Nichole Nordeman

ALBANY, NY
SEPTEMBER 23-24
Pepsi Arena
Sandi Patty,
Chonda Pierce

HARTFORD, CT
SEPT. 30 – OCT. 1
Hartford Civic Center
Sandi Patty,
Chonda Pierce,
Tammy Trent

SEATTLE, WA
OCTOBER 7-8
Key Arena
Sandi Patty,
Chonda Pierce,
Jennifer Rothschild

DES MOINES, IA
OCTOBER 14-15
Wells Fargo Arena
Sandi Patty,
Chonda Pierce,
Jennifer Rothschild

ST. PAUL, MN
OCTOBER 21-22
Xcel Energy Center
Sandi Patty,
Chonda Pierce,
Jennifer Rothschild

CHARLOTTE, NC
OCTOBER 28-29
Charlotte Coliseum
Sandi Patty, Beth Moore,
Sherri Shepherd

OKLAHOMA CITY, OK
NOVEMBER 4-5
Ford Center
Kristin Chenoweth,
Sandi Patty,
Chonda Pierce

ORLANDO, FL
NOVEMBER 11-12
TD Waterhouse Centre
Avalon,
Chonda Pierce,
Tammy Trent

1-888-49-FAITH womenoffaith.com